SELECTIONS FROM
THE SACRED WRITINGS OF THE SIKHS

UNESCO COLLECTION OF REPRESENTATIVE WORKS:
INDIAN SERIES

UNESCO COLLECTION OF REPRESENTATIVE WORKS:
INDIAN SERIES

This work is part of the Indian Series of the Translations Collection of the United Nations Educational, Scientific and Cultural Organization. It is published in accordance with an agreement between UNESCO and the Government of India, and as part of the Organization's 'Major Project' for furthering mutual appreciation of the cultural values of East and West.

SELECTIONS FROM
THE SACRED WRITINGS OF THE SIKHS

TRANSLATED BY

DR TRILOCHAN SINGH
BHAI JODH SINGH
KAPUR SINGH
BAWA HARKISHEN SINGH
KHUSHWANT SINGH

REVISED BY

GEORGE S. FRASER

INTRODUCTION BY

S. RADHAKRISHNAN

FOREWORD BY

ARNOLD TOYNBEE

SAMUEL WEISER, INC.
New York
1973

First American Edition 1973

Samuel Weiser, Inc.
734 Broadway
New York, New York 10003

© George Allen & Unwin Ltd., 1960

ISBN 0-87728-241-2 *hardback*
0-87728-120-3 *paperback*

Printed in Great Britain

To the Memory of
BHAI SAHIB
DR VIR SINGH
(b. December 5, 1872—d. June 10, 1957)

*who devoted his whole Life to
the exposition of Sikh Scriptures*

FOREWORD

by ARNOLD TOYNBEE

This translation is the first that has made the Adi Granth accessible, in more than short extracts, to the English-speaking public. Its publication is therefore an important event in the history of the now rapidly increasing contact between different peoples and civilizations in the fields of literature, religion, and other provinces of spiritual life. The Adi Granth is part of mankind's common spiritual treasure. It is important that it should be brought within the direct reach of as many people as possible. Few readers of English will have had the opportunity of hearing the Adi Granth being chanted in the Golden Temple of the Sikh religion at Amritsar; and few, again, of those who have heard the chanting have been in a position to understand its meaning. Here is the book in English. Readers of English can now not merely read it but ponder over it. A book that has meant, and means, so much to such a notable community as the Sikh Khalsa deserves close study from the rest of the world.

The Adi Granth is remarkable for several reasons. Of all known religious scriptures, this book is the most highly venerated. It means more to Sikhs than even the Qur'an means to Muslims, the Bible to Christians, and the Torah to Jews. The Adi Granth is the Sikhs' perpetual guru (spiritual guide). It was formally invested with this function by the last in the series of the human gurus that began with the founder of the Sikh religion, Nanak.

Perhaps Nanak himself would have modestly disclaimed the title of 'founder.' He might have preferred to say that he was merely bringing to light, and gathering together, the cardinal religious truths and precepts that had been scattered, in explicit form or implicitly, through the religious legacies of a number of forerunners of his. For Nanak the fundamental truth was that, for a human being, the approach to God lies through self-abnegation; and this is indeed the chief message of most of the higher religions that have made their appearance up to date.

Nearly all the higher religions that count in the world

today—in fact, all of them except Zoroastrianism—have originated in one or other of two regions: India and South-West Asia. The Indian and the Judaic religions are notoriously different in spirit; and, where they have met, they have sometimes behaved like oil and vinegar. Their principal meeting-ground has been India, where Islam has impinged on Hinduism violently. On the whole, the story of the relations between these two great religions on Indian ground has been an unhappy tale of mutual misunderstanding and hostility. Yet, on both sides of this religious barrier, there has been a minority of discerning spirits who have seen that, at bottom, Hinduism and Islam are each an expression of the same fundamental religious truth, and that these two expressions are therefore reconcilable with each other and are of supreme value when brought into harmony. The Sikh religion might be described, not inaccurately, as a vision of this Hindu-Muslim common ground. To have discovered and embraced the deep harmony underlying the historic Hindu-Muslim discord has been a noble spiritual triumph; and Sikhs may well be proud of their religion's êthos and origin.

This religion is the creation of ex-Hindu religious inquirers who adopted monotheism and rejected caste under the inspiration of Islam. The greater part of the Adi Granth consists of hymns written by Nanak and the gurus who succeeded him until the succession of human gurus was closed in favour of their holy book. But the Adi Granth is a catholic anthology. It also includes hymns written by earlier Indian seers in whom Nanak and his successors recognized kindred spirits; and some of these contributors to the Granth are Hindus, while others are Muslims. Their writings have found a place in the Adi Granth because the compilers of it held, and this surely with good reason, that these seers were Sikhs in fact, though they lived and wrote before the Sikh religion took institutional form. They were Sikhs because they brought out and emphasized the universal spiritual truths contained in their respective religious traditions; and these truths belong to all ages and to all faiths.

Mankind's religious future may be obscure; yet one thing can be foreseen: the living higher religions are going to influence each other more than ever before, in these days of increasing communication between all parts of the world and all branches of the human race. In this coming religious debate, the Sikh religion, and its scriptures the Adi Granth, will have something of special value to say to the rest of the world. This religion is itself a monument of creative spiritual intercourse between two traditional religions whose relations have otherwise not been happy. This is a good augury.

PREFACE

UNESCO entrusted the task of translating a selection of the Sacred Writings of the Sikhs to the Sahitya Akademi (Indian Academy of Letters). In pursuance of this mission the Akademi called a meeting of eminent Sikh Scholars, under the presidentship of Dr S. Radhakrishnan, Vice-President of the Indian Republic. Amongst those who attended the meeting and advised in the selection of translators and hymns was the venerable poet, the late Dr Bhai Vir Singh. A committee was set up under the chairmanship of S. B. Teja Singh, retired Chief Justice of High Court, and a panel of translators whose names appear in this book was chosen. Dr Trilochan Singh was the convener of this committee. The translations were revised from the point of view of English style by G. S. Fraser, working with Khushwant Singh.

This volume is the fruit of the joint labours of the most eminent Sikh theologians and scholars of the day and is the first publication of what might be described as an authorized English version of some of the Sacred Hymns of the Sikh scriptures.

UNESCO
Sahitya Akademi

CONTENTS

FOREWORD	9
PREFACE	13
INTRODUCTION	17

PART ONE
SELECTIONS FROM THE 'ĀDI GURU GRANTH'

1	*The Hymns of Guru Nanak*	27
2	*Hymns of Guru Angad Dev*	120
3	*Hymns of Guru Amar Das*	125
4	*Hymns of Guru Ram Das*	141
5	*Hymns of Guru Arjan Dev*	154
6	*Hymns of Guru Tegh Bahadur*	205
7	*Hymns of the 'Pre-Nānak Saints'*	211
8	*Hymns of the 'Contemporary Saints'*	248

PART TWO
SELECTIONS FROM THE 'DASM GRANTH'

9	*Hymns of Guru Gobind Singh*	266
GLOSSARY		276
INDEX		283

INTRODUCTION

The sudden widening of the spatial horizon has widened at the same time the horizons of the mind. There is an eagerness to know the ideas and beliefs by which other people live. This translation of a few selections from the *Ādi Granth* is a small attempt towards the better understanding of other peoples' ideas and convictions.

I

The *Ādi Granth*, which is regarded as the greatest work of Punjabi literature, is largely the work of Guru Arjan, the fifth of the ten Sikh Gurus.[1] He brought together the writings of the first four Gurus and those of the Hindu and Muslim saints from different parts of India. Guru Arjan's successors made a few additions and the tenth Guru, Gobind Singh, said that there would be no more Gurus and the *Granth* should be regarded as the living voice of all the prophets: *Guru-Vāṇī*. William Penn says: 'There is something nearer to us than scriptures, to wit, the word in the heart from which all scriptures come.' Japji says: '*gurmukh nādaṁ gurmukh vedaṁ*,' 'the Word of the Guru is the music which the seers hear in their moments of ecstasy; the Word of the Guru is the highest scripture. By communion with the Word we attain the vision unattainable.' Guru Arjan says that the BOOK is the abode of God: '*pothī paramesvar kā thān*.' The hymns are set to music. We find in *Ādi Granth* a wide range of mystical emotion, intimate expressions of the personal realization of God and rapturous hymns of divine love. The Sikh creed includes belief in the ten Gurus and the *Ādi Granth*.

A remarkable feature of the *Ādi Granth* is that it contains the writings of the religious teachers of Hinduism, Islam, etc.[2]

[1]
1. Guru Nānak, 1469–1539.
2. Guru Angad, 1504–1552.
3. Guru Amar Dās, 1479–1574.
4. Guru Ram Dās, 1534–1581.
5. Guru Arjan, 1563–1606.
6. Guru Har Govind, 1595–1644.
7. Guru Har Rai, 1630–1661.
8. Guru Harkishan, 1656–1664.
9. Guru Tegh Bahadur, 1621–1675.
10. Guru Gobind Singh, 1666–1708.

[2] The *Ādi Granth* includes hymns by Farid (twelfth century), Beni (twelfth century), Jaideva (twelfth century), Sadhna (thirteenth century), Trilochan (b. 1267), Nāmdeva (thirteenth century), Rāmānand (1360–1450), Sain (1390–1440), Pipa (b. 1425), Kabir (1440–1518), Ravidas (fifteenth century), Dhanna (early sixteenth century), Bhikan (d. 1573), Sūrdas (b. 1528), Parmānanda, a disciple of Ramanand.

This is in consistency with the tradition of India which respects all religions and believes in the freedom of the human spirit. Indian spiritual tradition is not content with mere toleration. There can be no goodwill or fellowship when we only tolerate each other. Lessing, in his *Nathan the Wise*, rebuked the habit of condescending toleration. We must appreciate other faiths, recognize that they offer rich spiritual experiences and encourage sacrificial living and inspire their followers to a noble way of life. The Sikh Gurus who compiled the *Ādi Granth* had this noble quality of appreciation of whatever was valuable in other religious traditions. The saints belong to the whole world. They are universal men, who free our minds from bigotry and superstition, dogma and ritual, and emphasize the central simplicities of religion. The great seers of the world are the guardians of the inner values who correct the fanaticisms of their superstitious followers.

The Hindu leaders neglected to teach the spiritual realities to the people at large who were sunk in superstition and materialism. Religion became confused with caste distinctions and taboos about eating and drinking. The Muslims were also victims of superstition and some of their leaders were afflicted with the disease of intolerance.[1] Saints arose in different parts of the country, intent on correcting the injustices and cruelties of society and redeeming it: Jnānesvar, Nāmdev, and Eknāth in Māhārāṣṭra, Narsingh Mehta in Gujerat, Caitanya in Bengal, Kabīr in Uttar Pradesh, Vallabhācārya in Āndhra and others. All these stirred the people with a new feeling of devotion, love and humanity. They stressed that one's religion was tested not by one's beliefs but by one's conduct. No heart which shuts out truth and love can be the abode of God.

At a time when men were conscious of failure, Nānak appeared to renovate the spirit of religion and humanity. He did not found a new faith or organize a new community. That was done by his successors, notably the fifth Guru. Nānak tried to build a nation of self-respecting men and women, devoted to God and their leaders, filled with a sense of equality and brotherhood for all.

[1] Nanak wrote: 'The age is a knife. Kings are butchers. They dispense justice when their palms are filled. Decency and laws have vanished, falsehood stalks abroad. Then came Babar to Hindustan. Death disguised as a Moghul made war on us. There was slaughter and lamentation. Did not thou, O Lord, feel the pain?'

The Gurus are the light-bearers to mankind. They are the messengers of the timeless. They do not claim to teach a new doctrine but only to renew the eternal wisdom. Nānak elaborated the views of the Vaiṣṇava saints. His best known work is *Jap Sahib* or *Japji*, the morning prayer. Guru Arjan's popular composition is *Sukhmaṇi*.

The Sikh Gurus transcend the opposition between the personal and the impersonal, between the transcendent and the immanent. God is not an abstraction but an actuality. He is Truth, formless nirguṇa, absolute, eternal, infinite, beyond human comprehension. He is yet revealed through creation and through grace to anyone who seeks Him through devotion. He is given to us as a Presence in worship. The ideas we form of Him are intellectualizations of that presence. A great Muslim saint observed: 'Who beholds me formulates it not and who formulates me beholds me not. A man who beholds and then formulates is veiled from me by the formulation.' It is the vice of theology to define rather than to express, to formulate rather than to image or symbolize the indefinable. Silence is the only adequate expression of that which envelops and embraces us. No word, however noble, no symbol, however significant, can communicate the ineffable experience of being absorbed in the dazzling light of the Divine. Light is the primal symbol we use, of a consciousness ineffably beyond the power of the human mind to define or limit. The unveiled radiance of the sun would be darkness to the eye that strives to look into it. We can know it only by reflection, for we are ourselves a part of its infinite awareness.

Muhammad adopted the rigid monotheism from Judaism. Thou shalt not make unto thee a graven image, nor any manner of likeness of anything that is in the heaven above or that is in the earth beneath, or that is in the water under the earth.[1] Rāmānanda was hostile to the worship of images. If God is a stone I will worship a mountain. Kabir says:

> The images are all lifeless, they cannot speak:
> I know, for I have cried aloud to them.
> The Purāṇa and the Qurān are mere words:
> Lifting up the curtain, I have seen.[2]

[1] Exodus xx. 3–4.
[2] Rabindranath Tagore's English translation.

Nānak was greatly impressed by the monotheism of Islam and denounced image worship. One God who is just, loving, righteous, who is formless and yet the creator of the universe, who desires to be worshipped through love and righteousness that is the belief that has dominated Sikhism. When at the temple of Jagannāth, Nānak saw the worship in which lights were waved before the image and flowers and incense were presented on gold salvers studded with pearls, he burst into song:

> The sun and moon, O Lord, are Thy lamps; the firmament
> Thy salver and the oils of the stars the pearls set therein.
> The perfume of the sandal tree is Thy incense; the wind
> Is Thy fan, all the forests are Thy flowers, O Lord of light.

God is not limited to any one incarnation but sends His messengers from time to time, to lead struggling humanity towards Him. It is the law of the spiritual world that whenever evil and ignorance darken human affairs, morality and wisdom will come to our rescue.[1]

The Guru is the indwelling Divine who teaches all through the gentle voice of conscience. He appears outside in human form to those who crave for a visible guide. The enlightener is the inner self. Nānak is, for the Sikhs, the voice of God arousing the soul to spiritual effort. Faith in the Guru is adopted by both the Hindus and the Muslim sufis. The latter emphasize the need of a religious teacher, Pir, to guide the initiate in prayer and meditation. The Gurus are human and not divine. They are not to be worshipped. Guru Gobind Singh says: 'Whosoever regards me as Lord shall be damned and destroyed ... I am but the servant of God.'

God alone is real. The world is real because God animates it and is found through it. The created world is not in an absolute sense. It arises from God and dissolves into Him. How came the Changeless to create a world of change? How did the One go forth into the many? If the one is compelled to create, it suffers from imperfection and insufficiency. But total perfection cannot have this insufficiency. The question assumes that the Eternal at one moment of time began the task of creation. But Eternity has no beginning and no end. If its nature is to

---

[1] See *Bhagavadgita* iv. 7-8. (With Sanskrit text, translation and commentary by S. Radhakrishnan; Allen & Unwin, London, 1948.)

create, it eternally creates. The idea of a God absorbed in self-contemplation and then for some unknown reason rousing Himself to create a universe is but a reflection of our human state. We alternate between activity and rest, between inertia and excitement. Divine beatitude consists in a simultaneous union of contemplation and of act of self-awareness and of self-giving. A static perfection is another name for death. Nānak looks upon the creative power of the Supreme as māyā. It is integral to the Supreme Being.

II

The way to the knowledge of God is through self-surrender. It is not ceremonial piety; it is something inward in the soul. Those who, in the humility of a perfect self-surrender, have ceased to cling to their own petty egos are taken over by the superhuman Reality, in the wonder of an indescribable love. The soul rapt in the vision and possession of a great loveliness grows to its likeness. Surrender to God becomes easy in the company of a saintly teacher, a Guru.

Man is a child of God. He is mortal when he identifies himself with the perishable world and body. He can become immortal through union with God; until then he wanders in the darkness of the world. He is like a spark from the fire or a wave of the ocean. The individual comes forth from God, is always in Him as a partial expression of His will and at last, when he becomes perfect, manifests God's will perfectly.

We have to tread the path which saints have trodden to direct union with the Divine. We have to tread the interior way, to pass through crises, through dark nights and ordeals of patience. Nānak says: 'Yoga is not the smearing of ashes, is not the ear-rings and shaven beard, not the blowing of conches but it is remaining unspotted amidst impurity, thus is the contact with Yoga gained.'

Nānak was critical of the formalism of both the Hindus and the Muslims. He went to bathe in the Ganges as is usual with devout Hindus. When the Hindus threw water towards the rising sun as an offering to their dead ancestors, Nānak threw water in the opposite direction. When questioned, he said: 'I am watering my fields in the Punjab. If you can throw water to the dead in heaven, it should be easier to send it to a place on earth.' On another occasion, he fell asleep with his feet towards Mecca. An outraged Mulla drew his attention to it. Nānak answered: 'If you think I show disrespect by having my feet towards the house of God, turn them in some other direction where God does not dwell.' Nānak says: 'To worship an image, to make a pilgrimage to a shrine, to remain in a desert, and yet have the mind impure is all in vain; to be saved, worship only the Truth.' Nānak tells us: 'Keep no feeling of enmity for anyone. God is contained in every bosom. Forgiveness is love at its highest power.' Nānak says: 'Where there is forgiveness there is God Himself.'

When Ajita Randhava asked Guru Nānak about ahiṁsā, Nānak replied:

(1) Do not wish evil for anyone. This is ahiṁsā of thought.
(2) Do not speak harshly of anyone. This is ahiṁsā of speech.
(3) Do not obstruct anyone's work. This is ahiṁsā of action.
(4) If a man speaks ill of you, forgive him.
(5) Practise physical, mental and spiritual endurance.
(6) Help the suffering even at the cost of your life.

Belief in a separate self and its sufficiency is the original sin. Self-noughting is the teaching of the seers of all religions. Jesus says: 'If any man would follow me, let him deny himself.' Meister Eckhart declared that the Kingdom of God is for none but the thoroughly dead. We should aim to escape from the prison of our selfhood and not to escape from the body which is the temple of God. Until we reach the end we will have other lives to pass through. No failure is final. An eventual awakening for all is certain.

Nānak and his followers believe in the doctrine of karma and rebirth. We are born with different temperaments. Some are greedy and possessive, others fretful and passionate. We come into the world bearing the impress of our past karma. Circumstances may stimulate these qualities. We may by our effort weaken the evil dispositions and strengthen the good ones. True happiness cannot be found in perishable things. It is found only in union with the Supreme. We are caught in the world of saṁsāra or change; in the wheel of births and deaths because we identify ourselves with the physical organism and the environment. We can be freed from the rotating wheel of saṁsāra by union with God attained through devotion. We must accept God as the guiding principle of our life. It is not necessary to renounce the world and become an ascetic. God is everywhere, in the field and the factory as in the cell and the monastery.

The Sikhs, like some other Vaiṣṇava devotees who preceded them, denounce caste distinctions. Rāmānanda said:

*Jāti panthi pūcchai nahi koi
hari ko bhaje so hari kā hoi.*

Let no one ask of caste or sect; if anyone worships God then he is God's. As God dwells in all creatures none is to be despised. When we become one with God through wholehearted surrender, we live our lives on earth as instruments of the Divine.

The aim of liberation is not to escape from the world of space and time but to be enlightened, wherever we may be. It is to live in this world knowing that it is divinely informed. To experience a timeless reality we need not run away from the world. For those who are no longer bound to the wheel of saṁsāra, life on earth is centred in the bliss of eternity. Their life is joy and where joy is, there is creation. They have no other country here below except the world itself. They owe their loyalty and love to the whole of humanity. God is universal. He is not the God of this race or that nation. He is the God of all human beings. They are all equal in His sight and can approach Him directly. We must, therefore, have regard for other peoples and other religions.

Nānak strove to bring Hindus and Muslims together. His life and teaching were a symbol of the harmony between the two communities. A popular verse describes him as a Guru for the Hindus and a Pir for the Muslims.

*Guru Nanak shah Fakir
Hindu kā Guru, Mussulman kā pīr.*

III

The transformation of the peaceful followers of Nānak into a militant sect was the work of the sixth Guru, Har Gobind ˙.d of Guru Gobind Singh, the tenth and last Guru. The tenth Guru converted the young community of disciples (Sikhs, śiṣyas) into a semi-military brotherhood with special symbols and sacraments for protecting them. When his father Guru

Tegh Bahadur was summoned by Emperor Aurangzeb who faced him with the alternative of conversion to Islam or death, he preferred death and left a message: I gave my head but not my faith.

sirr dīyā purr sirrar nā dīyā.

His four sons also gave their lives in defence of their faith.

On the New Year Day in 1669, Guru Gobind initiated five of his followers known as Panj Pyārās (five beloved ones), into a new fraternity called the Khalsa or the Pure. Of these five, one was a Brahmin, one a Kṣatriya and the others belonged to the lower castes. He thus stressed social equality. They all drank out of the same bowl and were given new names with the suffix Singh (Lion) attached to them. They resolved to observe the five K's, to wear their hair and beard unshorn (Keś),[1] to carry a comb in the hair (Kangha), to wear a steel bangle on the right wrist (Kara), to wear a pair of shorts (Kaccha), and to carry a sword (Kirpan). They were also enjoined to observe four rules of conduct (rahat), not to cut their hair, to abstain from smoking tobacco and avoid intoxicants, not to eat meat unless the animal has been slaughtered in the manner prescribed, and to refrain from adultery. A new script, a new scripture, new centres of worship, new symbols and ceremonies made Sikhism into a new sect, if not a new religion. What started as a movement of Hindu dissenters has now become a new creed.

It is, however, unfortunate that the barriers which the Sikh Guru laboured to cast down are again being re-created. Many pernicious practices against which they revolted are creeping into Sikh society. Worldly considerations are corrupting the great ideals. Religion which lives in the outer threshold of consciousness without conviction in the mind or love in the heart is utterly inadequate. It must enter into the structure of our life, become a part of our being. The Upaniṣad says: He alone knows the truth who knows all living creatures as himself. The barriers of seas and mountains will give way before the call of eternal truth which is set forth with freshness of feeling and fervour of devotion in the *Ādi Granth*.

S. RADHAKRISHNAN

New Delhi

[1] Some Hindu ascetics do not cut their hair and beards.

PART ONE

SELECTIONS FROM THE 'ĀDI GURU GRANTH'

I

THE HYMNS OF GURU NANAK
(1469-1539)

ੴ

Guru Nānak, the founder of Sikhism, was born at Talwandi, a small village forty miles from Lahore (now in Pakistan). He was a moody, meditative child and even in his schooldays preferred the company of itinerant holy men to that of his schoolmates. His interest in religious discourse persisted in his youth and he abandoned one trade after another in pursuit of truth, and ultimately made it his sole mission in life. He left his wife and sons, and with a Muslim companion called Mardana, he travelled far and wide visiting places of pilgrimage and seeking the company of scholars and divines. His travels took him as far as Assam in the East, Ceylon in the South, Mecca in the West and Tibet in the North, and brought him into contact with many people including the first Mughal Emperor Babur.

During the last fifteen years of life, Nānak settled down in the town of Kartarpur and preached his faith. The disciples that gathered round him—Shishyas—became the Sikhs (Punjabi version of the Sanskrit word.)

Although Nānak had two sons, he chose a devoted disciple to take his place as spiritual successor.

There are 974 hymns by Guru Nānak in the *Ādi Granth*.

I. THE JAPJI
OR, THE MEDITATION
(Morning Prayer)

ੴ

PROEM

ik oṅkār satnām kartā purkh

There is one God,
Eternal Truth is His Name;
Maker of all things,
Fearing nothing and at enmity with nothing,
Timeless is His Image;
Not begotten, being of His own Being:
By the grace of the Guru, made known to men.

Jap: The Meditation

AS HE WAS IN THE BEGINNING: THE TRUTH,
SO THROUGHOUT THE AGES,
HE EVER HAS BEEN: THE TRUTH,
SO EVEN NOW HE IS TRUTH IMMANENT,
SO FOR EVER AND EVER HE SHALL BE TRUTH ETERNAL.

1

socai soc nā hovaī je socī lakhvār

It is not through thought that He is to be comprehended
Though we strive to grasp Him a hundred thousand times;
Nor by outer silence and long deep meditation
Can the inner silence be reached;
Nor is man's hunger for God appeasable
By piling up world-loads of wealth.
All the innumerable devices of worldly wisdom
Leave a man disappointed; not one avails.

How then shall we know the Truth?
How shall we rend the veils of untruth away?
Abide thou by His Will, and make thine own,
His will, O Nānak, that is written in thy heart.

2

hukmī hovan ākār, hukam nā kehiā jāī

Through His Will He creates all the forms of things,
But what the form of His Will is, who can express?
All life is shaped by His ordering,
By His ordering some are high, some of low estate,
Pleasure and pain are bestowed as His Writ ordaineth.

Some through His Will are graciously rewarded,
Others must grope through births and deaths;
Nothing at all, outside His Will, is abiding.
O Nānak, he who is aware of the Supreme Will
Never in his selfhood utters the boast: 'It is I'.

3

gāvai ko tān hovai kisai tān

Those who believe in power,
Sing of His power;
Others chant of His gifts
As His messages and emblems;
Some sing of His greatness,
And His gracious acts;
Some sing of His wisdom
Hard to understand;
Some sing of Him as the fashioner of the body.
Destroying what He has fashioned;
Others praise Him for taking away life
And restoring it anew.

Some proclaim His Existence
To be far, desperately far, from us;
Others sing of Him
As here and there a Presence
Meeting us face to face.

To sing truly of the transcendent Lord
Would exhaust all vocabularies, all human powers of expression,
Myriads have sung of Him in innumerable strains.
His gifts to us flow in such plentitude
That man wearies of receiving what God bestows;
Age on unending age, man lives on His bounty;
Carefree, O Nānak, the Glorious Lord smiles.

4

sācā sāhib sāc nāe bhākhyā bhāu apār

The Lord is the Truth Absolute,
True is His Name.
His language is love infinite;
His creatures ever cry to Him;
'Give us more, O Lord, give more';
The Bounteous One gives unwearyingly.

What then should we offer
That we might see His Kingdom?
With what language
Might we His love attain?

In the ambrosial hours of fragrant dawn
Think upon and glorify
His Name and greatness.
Our own past actions
Have put this garment on us,
But salvation comes only through His Grace.

O Nanak, this alone need we know,
That God, being Truth, is the one Light of all.

5

thāpiā nā jāe kītā nā hoe

He cannot be installed like an idol,
Nor can man shape His likeness.
He made Himself and maintains Himself
On His heights unstained for ever;
Honoured are they in His shrine
Who meditate upon Him.

Sing thou, O Nānak, the psalms
Of God as the treasury
Of sublime virtues.
If a man sings of God and hears of Him,
And lets love of God sprout within him,
All sorrow shall depart;
In the soul, God will create abiding peace.

The Word of the Guru is the inner Music;
The Word of the Guru is the highest Scripture;
The Word of the Guru is all pervading.
The Guru is Śiva, the Guru is Vishnu and Brahma,
The Guru is the Mother goddess.

If I knew Him as He truly is
What words could utter my knowledge?
Enlightened by God, the Guru has unravelled one mystery
'There is but one Truth, one Bestower of life;
May I never forget Him.'

6

tīrath nhāvaṅ je tis bhāvāṅ

I would bathe in the holy rivers
If so I could win His love and grace;
But of what use is the pilgrimage
If it pleaseth Him not that way?

What creature obtains anything here
Except through previous good acts?
Yet hearken to the Word of the Guru
And his counsel within thy spirit
Shall shine like precious stone.

The Guru's divine illumination
Has unravelled one mystery;
There is but one Bestower of life
May I forget Him never.

7

je jug cārai ārjā hor dasūnī hoe

Were a man to live through the four ages,
Or even ten times longer,
Though his reputation were to spread over the nine shores,
Though the whole world were to follow in his train,
Though he were to be universally famous,
Yet lacking God's grace, in God's presence
Such a man would be disowned;
Such a man would be merely a worm among vermin
And his sins will be laid at his door.

On the imperfect who repent, O Nānak, God bestows virtue,
On the striving virtuous He bestows increasing blessedness.
But I cannot think there is any man so virtuous
Who can bestow any goodness on God.

8

suniai sidh pīr sur nāth

By hearkening to the Name
The disciple becomes a Master,
A guide, a saint, a seraph;
By hearkening to the Name
The earth, the bull that bears it
And the heavens are unveiled.

By hearkening to the Name
Man's vision may explore
Planets, continents, nether regions.
Death vexes not in the least
Those that hearken to the Name;
They are beyond Death's reach.

Saith Nānak, the saints are always happy;
By hearkening to the Name
Sorrow and sin are destroyed.

9

suniai īṣur barmā ind

By hearkening to the Name
Mortals obtain the godliness
Of Śiva, Brahma and Indra;
By hearkening to the Name
The lips of the lowly
Are filled with His praise.

By hearkening to the Name
The art of Yoga and all the secrets
Of body and mind are unveiled.
By hearkening to the Name
The Vedic wisdom comes,
And also the knowledge of the shastras and smritis.

Saith Nānak, the saints are always happy;
By hearkening to the Name
Sorrow and sin are destroyed.

10

suniai sat santokh gyān

Hearkening to the Name bestows
Truth, divine wisdom, contentment.
To bathe in the joy of the Name
Is to bathe in the holy places.

By hearing the Name and reading it
A man attains to honour;
By hearkening, the mind may reach
The highest blissful poise
Of meditation on God.

Saith Nānak, the saints are always happy;
By hearkening to the Name
Sorrow and sin are destroyed.

11

suniai sarā gunā ke gāh

By hearkening to the Name,
Man dives deep in an ocean of virtues;
By hearkening to the Name
The disciple becomes an apostle,
A prelate, a sovereign of souls.

By hearkening to the Name
The blind man sees the way;
By hearkening to the Name
Impassable streams are forded.

Saith Nānak, the saints are always happy;
By hearkening to the Name
Sorrow and sin are destroyed.

12

manain kī gat kahī nā jāe

Of him who truly believes in the Name
Words cannot express the condition;
He himself will later repent
Should he ever try to describe it;
No pen, no paper, no writer's skill
Can get anywhere really near it.

Such is the power of His stainless Name,
He who truly believes in it, knows it.

13

manain surt hovai man budh

Through belief in the Name
The mind soars high into enlightenment.
The whole universe stands self-revealed.
Through inner belief in the Name
One avoids ignorant stumbling;
In the light of such a faith
The fear of death is broken.

Such is the power of His stainless Name,
He who truly believes in it, knows it.

14

manaiṅ mārag ṭhāk nā pāe

Nothing can bar or mar the paths
Of those who truly believe in the Name,
They depart from here with honour;
They do not lose the proper path.
The spirit of those imbued with faith
Is wedded to realization of truth.

Such is the power of His stainless Name,
He who truly believes in it, knows it.

15

manaiṅ pāvai mokh dūar

Those who have inner belief in the Name,
Always achieve their own liberation,
Their kith and kin are also saved.
Guided by the light of the Guru
The disciple steers safe himself,
And many more he saves;
Those enriched with inner belief
Do not wander begging.

Such is the power of His stainless Name,
He who truly believes in it, knows it.

16

pañc parvān pañc pardhān

His chosen are His saints, and great are they,
Honoured are the saints in the court of God;
The saints add lustre to the courts of the Lord.
Their minds are fixed upon the Guru alone.

All that they say is wisdom, but by what wisdom
Can we number the works of the Lord?
The mythical bull is *dharma:* the offspring of Compassion
That holds the thread on which the world is strung.

Even a little common sense makes one understand this:
How could a bull's shoulders uphold the earth?
There are so many earths, planets on planet.
What is that bears these burdens?

One ever-flowing pen inscribed the names
Of all the creatures, in their kinds and colours;
But which of us would seek to pen that record,
Or if we could, how great the scroll would be.

How can one describe Thy beauty and might of Thy Works?
And Who has power to estimate Thy Bounty, O Lord?
All creation emerging from Thy One Word,
Flowing out like a multitude of rivers.

How can an insignificant creature like myself
Express the vastness and wonder of Thy creation?
I am too petty to have anything to offer Thee;
I cannot, even once, be sacrifice unto Thee.

To abide by Thy Will, O Formless One, is man's best offering;
Thou who art Eternal, abiding in Thy Peace.

17

asaṅkh jap asaṅkh bhau

There is no counting of men's prayers,
There is no counting their ways of adoration.
Thy lovers, O Lord, are numberless;
Numberless those who read aloud from the Vedas;
Numberless those Yogis who are detached from the world;

Numberless are Thy Saints contemplating,
Thy virtues and Thy wisdom;
Numberless are the benevolent, the lovers of their kind.

Numberless Thy heroes and martyrs
Facing the steel of their enemies;
Numberless those who in silence
Fix their deepest thoughts upon Thee;

How can an insignificant creature like myself
Express the vastness and wonder of Thy creation?
I am too petty to have anything to offer Thee;
I cannot, even once, be a sacrifice unto Thee.
To abide by Thy Will, O Lord, is man's best offering;
Thou who art Eternal, abiding in Thy Peace.

18

asankh mūrakh andh ghor

There is no counting fools, the morally blind;
No counting thieves and the crooked,
No counting the shedders of the innocent blood;
No counting the sinners who go on sinning;

No counting the liars who take pleasure in lies;
No counting the dirty wretches who live on filth;
No counting the calumniators
Who carry about on their heads their loads of sin.

Thus saith Nānak, lowliest of the lowly:
I am too petty to have anything to offer Thee;
I cannot, even once, be a sacrifice unto Thee.
To abide by Thy Will, O Lord, is man's best offering;
Thou who art Eternal, abiding in Thy Peace.

19

asankh nām asankh thām

Countless are Thy Names, countless Thine abodes;
Completely beyond the grasp of the imagination
Are Thy myriad realms;
Even to call them myriad is foolish.

Yet through words and through letters
Is Thy Name uttered and Thy praise expressed;
In words we praise Thee,
In words we sing of Thy virtues.

It is in the words that we write and speak about Thee,
In words on man's forehead
Is written man's destiny,
But God who writes that destiny
Is free from the bondage of words

As God ordaineth, so man receiveth.
All creation is His Word made manifest;
Except in the Light of His Word
There is no way.

How can an insignificant creature like myself
Express the vastness and wonder of Thy creation?
I am too petty to have anything to offer Thee;
I cannot, even once, be a sacrifice unto Thee.
To abide by Thy Will, O Lord, is man's best offering;
Thou who art Eternal, abiding in Thy Peace.

20

bharīai hath pair tan deh

When the hands, feet and other parts
Of the body are besmeared with filth,
They are cleansed with water;
When a garment is defiled
It is rinsed with soapsuds;
So when the mind is polluted with sin,
We must scrub it in love of the Name.

We do not become sinners or saints,
By merely saying we are;
It is actions that are recorded;
According to the seed we sow, is the fruit we reap.
By God's Will, O Nānak,
Man must either be saved or endure new births.

21

tīrath tap dayā dat dān

Pilgrimages, penances, compassion and almsgiving
Bring a little merit, the size of sesame seed.
But he who hears and believes and loves the Name
Shall bathe and be made clean
In a place of pilgrimage within him.

All goodness is Thine, O Lord, I have none;
Though without performing good deeds
None can aspire to adore Thee.
Blessed Thou the Creator and the Manifestation,
Thou art the word, Thou art the primal Truth and Beauty,
And Thou the heart's joy and desire.

When in time, in what age, in what day of the month or week
In what season and in what month did'st Thou create the world?
The Pundits do not know or they would have written it in the Purāṇas;
The Qazis do not know, or they would have recorded it in the Koran;
Nor do the Yogis know the moment of the day,
Nor the day of the month or the week, nor the month nor the season.
Only God Who made the world knows when He made it.

Then how shall I approach Thee, Lord?
In what words shall I praise Thee?
In what words shall I speak of Thee?
How shall I know Thee?
O Nānak, all men speak of Him, and each would be wiser than the next man;
Great is the Lord, great is His Name,
What He ordaineth, that cometh to pass,
Nānak, the man puffed up with his own wisdom
Will get no honour from God in the life to come.

22

patālā patāl lakh agāsā agās

There are hundreds of thousands of worlds below and above ours,
And scholars grow weary of seeking for God's bounds.
The Vedas proclaim with one voice that He is boundless.
The Semitic Books mention eighteen hundred worlds;
But the Reality behind all is the One Principle.

If it could be written, it would have been,
But men have exhausted themselves in the effort;
O Nānak, call the Lord Great;
None but He knoweth, how great He is.

23

sālāhī sālāh etī surt nā pāīai

Thy praisers praise Thee,
And know not Thy greatness;
As rivers and streams flow into the sea,
But know not its vastness.

Kings who possess dominions vast as the sea,
With wealth heaped high as the mountain,
Are not equal to the little worm
That forgetteth not God in its heart.

24

ant nā siftī kehan nā ant

Infinite is His Goodness, and infinite its praise;
Infinite are His Works and infinite His gifts;
Where are the bounds of His seeing or His hearing?
Unfathomable is the infinity of His Mind;
There are no bounds even to His creation.

How many vex their hearts to know His limits
But seeking to explore Infinity, can find no bounds;
The more we say, the more there is left to say;
High is our Lord and very High is His throne;
His holy Name is higher than the highest.

He that would know His height, must be of the same height;
Only the Lord knoweth the greatness of the Lord.
Saith Nānak, only by God's grace and bounty
Are God's gifts bestowed on man.

25

bahutā karm likhiā nā jāe

Of His bounty one cannot write enough;
He is the great Giver, Who covets nothing;
How many mighty warriors beg at His door;
How many others, in numbers beyond reckoning.

Many waste His gifts in idle pleasure,
Many receive His gifts and yet deny Him;
Many are the fools who merely eat,
Many are always sorrowing and hungering;
Sorrow and hunger are also Thy gifts.

Liberation from bondage depends upon Thy Will;
There is no one to gainsay it;
Should a fool wish to,
Suffering will teach him wisdom.

The Lord knoweth what to give and He giveth;
Few acknowledge this. Those on whom He bestows,
O Nānak, the gift of praising Him and adoring Him
Are the true Kings of Kings.

26

amul gun amul vāpār

Priceless are His attributes,
Priceless His dealings;
Priceless the stores of His virtues,
Priceless the dealers in them;
Priceless those who seek these gifts,
Priceless those who take these gifts.

Pricelessly precious is devotion to Thee,
Pricelessly precious is absorption in Thee;
Priceless His Law and spirit of righteousness,
Priceless His Mansions of dispensation;
Priceless His scales of judgement,
Priceless His weights for judging.

Priceless His gifts,
Priceless His marks upon them;
Priceless His Mercy and priceless His Will;
How beyond price He is cannot be expressed.
Those who try to express it,
Are mute in adoration.

The Vedas proclaim Him,
So do the readers of the Purāṇas;
The learned speak of Him in many discourses;
Brahma and Indra speak of Him,
Śivas speak of Him, Siddhas speak of Him,
The Buddhas He has created, proclaim Him.

The demons and the gods speak of Him,
Demigods, men, sages and devotees
All try to describe Him;
Many have tried and still try to describe Him;
Many have spoken of Him and departed.

If as many people as lived in all the past
Were now to describe Him each in His own way,
Even then He would not be adequately described.

The Lord becometh as great as He wishes to be.
If anyone dares to claim that he can describe Him,
Write him down as the greatest fool on earth.

27

sodar terā kehā so ghar kehā

Where is the gate, where the mansion
From whence Thou watchest all creation,
Where sounds of musical melodies,
Of instruments playing, minstrel singing,
Are joined in divine harmony?
In various measures celestial musicians sing of Thee.

There the breezes blow, the waters run and the fires burn,
There Dharmrāj, the king of death, sits in state;
There the recording angels Chitra and Gupta write
For Dharmrāj to read and adjudicate;
There are the gods Īśvara and Brahma,
The goddess Pārvatī adorned in beauty,
There Indra sits on his celestial throne
And lesser gods, each in his place;
One and all sing of Thee.

There ascetics in deep meditation,
Holy men in contemplation,
The pure of heart, the continent,
Men of peace and contentment,
Doughty warriors never yielding
Thy praises ever singing.

From age to age, the pundit and the sage
Do Thee exalt in their studies;
There maidens fair, heart bewitching,
Who inhabit the earth, the upper and the lower regions,
Thy praises chant in their singing.

By the gems that Thou didst create,
In the sixty-eight places of pilgrimage
Is Thy Name exalted;

By warriors strong and brave in strife,
By the sources four from whence came life,
Of egg or womb, of sweat or seed,
Is Thy Name magnified.

The regions of the earth, the heavens and the Universe
That Thou didst make and dost sustain,
Sing to Thee and praise Thy Name.
Only those Thou lovest and have Thy grace
Can give Thee praise and in Thy love be steeped.

Others too there must be who Thee acclaim,
I have no memory of knowing them
Nor of knowledge, O Nānak, make a claim.
He alone is the Master true, Lord of the Word, ever the same.
He who made creation, is, shall be and shall ever remain;
He who made things of diverse species, shapes and hues,
Beholds that His handiwork His greatness proves.

What He Wills He ordains,
To Him no one can an order give,
For He, O Nānak, is the King of Kings,
As He Wills so we must live.

28

mundā santokh saram pat jholī

Going forth a begging,
Let contentment be thine earings,
Modesty thy begging bowl,
Smear thy body with ashes of meditation,
Let contemplation of death be thy beggar's rags;

Let thy body be chaste, virginal, clean,
Let faith in God be the staff on which thou leanest;
Let brotherhood with every man on earth
Be the highest aspiration of your Yogic Order.
Know that to subdue the mind
Is to subdue the world.

Hail, all hail unto Him,
Let your greetings be to the Primal God;
Pure and without beginning, changeless,
The same from age to age.

29

bhugat gyān dayā bhaṅdāran

Let knowledge of God be thy food,
Let mercy keep thy store,
And listen to the Divine Music
That beats in every heart.

He is the supreme Master,
He holdeth the nosestring of creation;
In the secret powers and magics,
There is no true savour.

Union with God and separation from Him
Are according to His Will,
What each gets is his meed.

Hail, all hail unto Him,
Let your greetings be to the Primal Lord;
Pure and without beginning, changeless,
The same from age to age.

30

ekā māī jugat vyāī

Māyā, the mythical goddess,
Sprang from the One, and her womb brought forth
Three acceptable disciples of the One:
Brahma, Viṣṇu and Śiva.
Brahma, it is said bodies forth the world,
Viṣṇu it is who sustains it;
Śiva the destroyer who absorbs,
He controls death and judgement.

God makes them to work as He wills,
He sees them ever, they see Him not:
That of all is the greatest wonder.

Hail, all hail unto Him,
Let your greetings be to the Primal Lord;
Pure and without beginning, changeless,
The same from age to age.

31

āsan loe loe bhaṅdār

God has His seat everywhere,
His treasure houses are in all places.
Whatever a man's portion is
God at the creation
Apportioned him that share once and for all.
What He has created
The Lord for ever contemplates.
O Nānak, true are His works
As He Himself is the True.

Hail, all hail unto Him,
Let your greetings be to the Primal Lord;
Pure and without beginning, changeless,
The same from age to age.

32

ik dū jībhau lakh hoe

Let my tongue become a hundred thousand tongues,
Let the hundred thousand be multiplied twenty-fold,
With each tongue many hundred thousands of times
I would repeat the holy Name of the Lord;
Thus let the soul step by step
Mount the stairs to the Bridegroom
And become one with Him.

On hearing of heavenly things,
He who can only crawl also longs to fly.
By God's grace alone, saith Nānak, is God to be grasped.
All else is false, all else is vanity.

33

ākhan jor nā cupe jor

Ye have no power to speak or in silence listen,
To ask or to give away;
Ye have no power to live or die,
Ye have no power to acquire wealth and dominion and be vain,.
Ye have no power to compel the mind to thought or reason,
He who hath the power, He creates and sees;
O Nānak, before the Lord there is no low or high degree.

34

ratī rutī thitī vār

God made the night and the day,
The days of the week and the months,
And He made the seasons;
He made winds to blow and water to run,
He made fire, He made the lower regions;
In the midst of all this He set the earth as a temple,
On it He set a diversity of creatures,
Various in kind and colour
Endless the number of their names.

All these lives are judged by their actions.
God is True and in His Court is truth dispensed;
There the elects are acceptable to Him,
And by His grace and His mercy
Honoured in His presence.
In that Court the bad shall be sifted from the good
When we reach His Court, O Nānak
We shall know this to be true.

35

dharam khaṅd kā eho dharam

I have described the realm of *dharma*,
Now I shall describe the realm of Knowledge;

How many are the winds, the fires, the waters,
How many are the Krishṇas and Śivas,
How many are the Brahmas fashioning the worlds,
Of many kinds and shapes and colours;
How many worlds, like our own there are,
Where action produces the consequences.

How many holy mountains to be climbed,
With how many sages, like Dhruva's teacher, Nārada
On the top of them.
How many adepts, Buddhas and Yogis are there,
How many goddesses and how many the images of the goddesses;
How many gods and demons and how many sages;

How many hidden jewels in how many oceans,
How many the sources of life;
How many the modes and diversities of speech,
How many are the kings, the rulers and the guides of men;
How many the devoted there are, who pursue this divine knowledge,
His worshippers are numberless, saith Nānak.

36

gyān khaṅd mai gyān parcaṅd

As in the realm of Knowledge wisdom shines forth,
And Music is heard from which myriad joys proceed;
So in the realm of Spiritual endeavour
The presiding deity is Beauty.
All things are shaped there incomparably,
The beauty of the place is beyond description;

And whoever even attempts to describe it,
Will certainly afterwards feel deep remorse:
Understanding, discernment, the deepest wisdom is fashioned there.
There are created the gifts of the sages and the seers.

37

karam khaṅd kī bānī jor

In the realm of Grace, spiritual power is supreme,
Nothing else avails;
There dwell doughty warriors brave and strong,
In whom is the Lord's Spirit,
And who by His praise are blended in Him.
Their beauty is beyond telling,
In their hearts the Lord dwelleth,
They do not die and they are not deceived.

There dwell also the congregations of the blessed,
In bliss they dwell, with the true one in their hearts.

In the realm of Truth,
Dwelleth the Formless One
Who, having created, watcheth His creation
And where He looks upon them with Grace;
And His creatures are happy.

All continents, worlds and universes
Are contained in this supreme realm;
Were one to strive to make an account of them all,
There would be no end to the count.

World there is on world there, form upon form there,
And all have their functions as God's will ordaineth;
The Lord seeth His creation and seeing it He rejoiceth.
O Nānak, the telling is hard, as iron is hard to hand.

38

jat pahārā dhīraj suniār

In the forge of continence,
Let patience be the goldsmith,
On the anvil of understanding
Let him strike with the hammer of knowledge;

Let the fear of God be the bellows,
Let austerities be the fire,
Let the love of God be the crucible,
Let the nectar of life be melted in it;

Thus in the mint of Truth,
A man may coin the Word,
This is the practice of those
On whom God looks with favour.
Nānak, our gracious Lord
With a glance makes us happy.

Epilogue

pavan gurū panī pitā

Air like the Guru's Word gives us the breath of life,
Water sires us, earth is our mother.
Day and night are the two nurses
That watch over the world,
And in whose lap we all play.

On good as well as our bad deeds
Shall be read His judgement;
As we have acted,
Some of us shall be near to God
Some of us far away.

Those that have meditated
On the Holy Name,
And have departed, their task completed,
Their faces are those of shining ones and, O Nānak,
How many they bring to liberty in their train.

II. SODAR—REHIRĀS
(*Evening Prayer*)

ੴ

1

sodar terā kehā so ghar kehā

(*This, the First Hymn of the Evening Prayer is the same as the Twenty-Seventh Hymn of the Japji, page 44*)

2

SPAKE GURU NĀNAK

sun vadā ākhai sabh koe

On hearing of the Lord,
All men speak of His greatness;
Only he that hath seen Him
Can know how great is He.
Who can conceive of His worth
Or who can describe Him?
Those who seek to describe Thee
Are lost in Thy depths.

O Great Lord, of depth unfathomable,
Ocean of virtues!
Who knoweth the bounds of Thy shores?
All the contemplatives
Have met and sought to contemplate Thee;
All the weighers of worth
Have met and sought to weigh Thy worth;
All the theologians and the mystics,
All the preachers and their teachers
Have not been able to grasp
One jot of Thy greatness.

All truths, all fervent austerities, every excellent act,
Every sublime achievement of the adepts,
Are Thy gifts, O Lord: without Thee
No man could attain perfection;
But where Thou hast granted Thy grace to a man,
Nothing can stand in his way.

How vain are the words of those that seek to praise Thee,
Thy treasuries are already filled with Thy praises;
He to whom Thou givest freely,
What should he do but praise Thee?

Saith Nānak: The True One is He
From whom all perfection springs.

3

SPAKE GURU NĀNAK

ākhaṅ jīvaṅ visraiṅ mar jāuṅ

If I remember Him I live,
If I forget Him I die;
Hard very hard indeed it is
To contemplate His Name;
If a man hungers after His Name
In that holy hunger
He consumeth all His pains.
True is the Lord
True is His Name.
O Mother, how can He be forgotten?

Even in praising a tiny part of His Name
Men grow weary but His true worth is not weighed;
If all men were to meet, and begin to try to exalt Him,
He would grow neither greater nor lesser by their praise.
He does not die, He does not suffer sorrow;
Ever He giveth, and never His store faileth.
This is the greatest wonder in Him,
That there never was nor there ever will be,
Another like to the Lord.

As great as Thou Thyself art, O my Lord,
So great are Thy gifts; as Thou madest the day,
So Thou madest the night also.
He who forgets Thee is low born
O Nānak: without His Name
Man is like the lowest of the outcasts.

4

SPAKE GURU RĀM DĀS

har ke jan satgur satpurkhā

O Servant of God, True Guru, Truth's true embodiment:
We that are low worms, seek our refuge in thee;
Mercifully bestow on us the light of the True Name.

O my friend, my divine Guru! set alight His Name within me;
The Name taught by my Guru is the help of my soul;
The praise of the Lord is my vocation;
Happy, most happy are the Lord's people,
Who have faith in the Lord, who thirst for Him,
And with the gift of His Name their thirst is slaked.
Then in the company of the blessed: they exalt His virtues.

Unhappy, most unhappy are those,,
To whom is not granted the sweet savour of His Name;
Death is their portion
Who have not sought their refuge
With the True Guru;
Nor have come to the congregation of the saints;
Accursed be their lives,
Accursed be the hopes they set on living.

The blessed who have entered into the companionship
Of the True Guru,
Are those on whose foreheads from the very beginning
This blessed fate was written.
Hail, hail to the holy congregation
In whose midst is the sweet savour of the Lord;
In the company of the saints, O Nānak,
The Lord sheddeth the true Light of His Name.

5

SPAKE GURU ARJAN

kahe re man citvai udam

O my soul, why art thou busy and troubled
When thou knowest the Lord will provide?
In the rocks and stones He hath set living creatures,
He putteth their food before them.

Beloved Lord, they who fall in with the company
　of the blessed,
Shall obtain their liberation.
By the grace of the Guru
They shall attain the state supreme;
Yea, though they were as the dry tree
They shall again be green.

Not on thy father or mother,
Not on the friends of thy household,
Not on thy wife nor on thy son,
Darest thou lean for thy daily bread:
The Lord provideth all
Why have fear in the mind.

The migrating cranes fly hundreds of miles,
They leave their young behind them.
Think, O Man: who feedeth the young birds?

God holdeth as in His palm
All the treasures of the world
And all the eighteen occult powers;
O Nānak, for ever and ever
Make thy heart a sacrifice unto Him.
There is no end or limit to His Being.

6

SPAKE GURU RĀM DĀS

so purkh nirañjan hari purkh nirañjan

That Being is Pure; He is without stain;
He is Infinite and beyond comprehension;
All worship Thee, all bow to Thee:
Thou who art Truth and the Creator.
All creatures are Thine, for all of them Thou provideth;
O saint, meditate on the Lord: who makes sorrow to be forgotten;
He Himself is the Lord, He Himself is the worshipper;
O Nānak, how insignificant is man.

Thou, O Lord, O One Supreme Being!
Thou art in every heart and soul,
Thou pervadest all things:
Some men beg for alms, some bestow them,
All this is the great game Thou playest.
It is Thou who givest and enjoyest the gifts,
I know of none other beside Thee.
Thou art the utterly Transcendent:
Infinite art Thou! Infinite art Thou!
How can I describe Thy attributes?
Unto those who serve and worship Thee truly
Nānak is a humble sacrifice.

They who think on Thee, they who meditate on Thee,
In this dark age have their peace.
They who think on Thee: they are saved, they are liberated;
For them death's noose is broken.

Those who meditate on the Fearless One
Will lose all their fear;
Those who have worshipped the Lord,
In the Lord they are now mingled.
Blest and blest again are those
That have set their thoughts on the Lord.
The humble Nānak is a sacrifice unto them.

O Lord, Thy inexhaustible treasure
Is filled and refilled with Thy worship;
O many and innumerable are the saints who adore Thee,
Manifold are their devotions;
They practise austerities and endlessly repeat Thy Name,
How many read the Smrities and Shastras, perform the six Hindu Observances.
But only those are truly saints
Who have won the love of my Lord.
Thou art the Primal Being, the Creator:
None setteth bounds on Thee, there is none other so great;
From age to age one and the same:
Ever and ever art Thou the same: Immovable Creator.
Whatever Thou willest, it is,
As Thou actest, so Thy acts prevaileth.
It is Thou who createst all things
And by whose command all things pass away.
Nānak singeth the praises of the Maker: the All-knowing.

7

SPAKE GURU RĀM DĀS

tū kartā saciār maiṅdā sāiṅ

Lord, Creator and Truth,
As Thy Will is, it is done; as Thou givest I receive;
All that is, is Thine: all men adore Thee;
Those whom Thou favourest have gotten the jewel of Thy Name.
The enlightened have sought it; the self-willed have lost it;
It is Thou who settest apart and Thou who unitest.

Thou art the Ocean: all things are within Thee,
There is none other beside Thee.
All the living are merely the game Thou playest;
By Thee, having fallen apart, one is set apart;
By Thee, being in union, one is united.

He whom Thou makest to know Thee, he knoweth Thee
And his mouth shall be for ever full of Thy praises;

He who has truly served the Lord is happy
And with ease is absorbed into the Divine Name.

Thou art the Creator: all that is, is Thy handiwork;
There is none other beside Thee.
What Thou createst, that Thou seest and knowest.
Through the Guru, saith Nānak,
Thou art revealed in Thy Truth.

8

SPAKE GURU NĀNAK

tit sarvaṛde bhaī lai nivāsā

Man, thou dwellest in the world that is as a pool,
Whose waters God hath made as hot as fire.
Stuck in the mire of worldly love, thy feet cannot move forward,
I have seen people drowning in this swamp.
O heart, O foolish heart, why thinkest thou not on the One?
Through forgetting thy Lord, thy virtues have melted away.

I am not chaste nor honest, I am not even a scholar;
Foolish and ignorant I came into the world,
O Lord, Nānak prayeth ever to seek
The sanctuary of their gathering
Who have not forgotten Thee.

9

SPAKE GURU ARJAN

bhaī parāpat mānukh dehuriā

Thou hast acquired this human frame,
This is thy opportunity to be one with God;
All other labours are unprofitable.
Seek the company of the holy and glorify His Name.
Strenuously prepare to cross this terrible ocean.
Thy life is being wasted
In love of the world's illusions.

I have not repeated His Name,
Nor made penance, practised austerities, nor been pious;
I have not served my Lord's saints nor thought of Him.
Nānak saith, my acts have been low;
Preserve me from shame O Lord,
Since I take my shelter in Thee.

III. SOHILĀ—ĀRTĪ
(Bed Time Prayer)

ੴ

I

SPAKE GURU NĀNAK

jai ghar kīrat ākhīai karte kā hoe vicāro

In the house in which men sing the Lord's praises
And meditate upon Him,
In that house sing the songs of praise
And remember the Creator;
Sing the song of praise of thy fearless Lord,
Let me be a sacrifice unto that song,
By which we attain everlasting solace.

Day by day, ever and ever,
He watcheth over His living creatures;
The Bountiful Giver looks after one and all.
Who can set a price on His gifts,
Or say how great is He.

The year and the sacred day for the wedding is fixed,
Comrades! pour oil at the door to welcome the bride;
Give me your blessings, O friends,
I depart for my union with God.

The summons is sent to every house,
To every soul, every day, it is issued;
Remember, O Nānak, Him who sends the summons,
The day is not far when you also may hear it.

2

SPAKE GURU NĀNAK

che ghar che gur che updeṣ

Six the systems, six their teachers,[1]
And six their different teachings:
The Lord of them all is the One Lord
However various His aspects are;
O brother, follow that system
That sings the Lord's praises:
There thy true glory lies.

Seconds, minutes, hours, quarters of a day;
Lunar and solar days make up a month,
Yet there are many times and many seasons;
One single sun runs through them all.
O Nānak, Thy Lord is likewise One,
However various His aspects are.

3

SPAKE GURU NĀNAK: THE ARTĪ

gagan mai thāl ravi cand dīpak banai

The firmament is Thy salver,
The sun and the moon Thy lamps;
The galaxy of stars are as pearls scattered,
The woods of sandal are Thine incense.
The breezes blow Thy royal fan;
The flowers of the forests,
Lie as offerings at Thy feet.
What wonderful worship with lamps is this
O Thou destroyer of fear!
Unstruck Music is the sound of Thy temple drums.

---

[1] Guru Nānak says that Divine Wisdom is like the Sun and the six Hindu systems are like the seasons.

Thousands are Thine eyes,
And yet Thou hast no eyes;
Thousands are Thy shapes,
And yet Thou hast no shape;
Thousands are Thy pure feet,
And yet Thou hast not one foot;
Thousands are Thy noses
And yet Thou hast no nose.

All this is Thy play and bewitches me.
In every heart there is light:
That light art Thou.
By the Light that is of God Himself
Is every soul illumined:
But this divine Light becomes manifest
Only by the Guru's teachings.
What is pleasing to Thee, O Lord
Is the best *arti*: worship with the lamps.

O Lord, my mind yearns for Thy lotus feet,
As the honey-bee for the nectar of the flowers.
Night and day Lord, I am athirst for Thee,
Give water of Thy mercy to Nānak:
He is like the sārang: the hawk-cuckoo that drinks only rain drops
So that he may dwell ever in the peace of Thy Name.

4

SPAKE GURU RĀM DĀS

kām krodh nagar bahu bhariā

With lust and with anger,
The city, that is thy body
Is full to the brim.
Meet as saint and destroy
That lust and that anger.
By God's decree
I have found my Guru

And my soul is absorbed
In the love of My Lord.
Bow humbly to the saint
That is a pious act.
Bow to the ground before him
That is devotion, indeed.

The faithless know not,
The joy of the love of the Lord;
In their hearts
Is the thorn of self-love,
And each step they take,
It pierces deeper and deeper
And they feel pain and sorrow
Till they bring death on their heads.

The Lord's chosen are absorbed in the Lord's Name.
The pain of birth and the fear of death are broken.
They have attained the Imperishable Lord;
Great honour is theirs in all regions.

I am poor and wretched,
But I am Thine, O Lord:
Save me, O save me
Thou greatest of the great.
Thy Name, to Thy slave Nānak
Is as his staff and his shield.
Only in the Name of the Lord
I have found my comfort.

5

SPAKE GURU ARJAN

karoṅ bentī suno mere mītā

I supplicate thee, my friend, to listen to me,
Here and now is the time to serve the saints;
Here, in this world, acquire the gain of godliness;
Thou shalt have ease enough in the world to come.

By day and by night the sum of the days decreaseth:
Seek the True Guru and balance thine accounts.

The world is awry, is illusionary. The man
Who knoweth God, the Brahm-jñani, is saved.
Whom God awakeneth to drink of His Name's essence,
He knoweth the Unknowable, whose story can never be told.

Strive to seek that
For which thou hast come into the world,
And through the grace of the Guru
God will dwell in thy heart.
Thou shalt abide in His Presence,
In comfort and in peace
And not return ever
To be born and to die once more.

O God, Searcher of hearts,
O God, who dispensest to each of us
The fruits of our acts,
Fulfil one wish of my heart:
Nānak, thy slave, craveth
The boon that he may be made
The dust that clings to the soles
Of the feet, O Lord, of the saints.

IV. OTHER HYMNS OF GURU NANAK

I

motī tā mandir usrai ratnī tā hoe jaḍāo

Though the outer wall of thy palace be made of pearls,
Though it be studded with gems,
Though the inner walls be smeared with musk
And fragrant with sandal and agar wood,
Commingling with sweet saffron's smell;
If these thy mind bewitch,
Beware, Man, lest thou forget
And remember not the Name of God.
God unremembered, life runs to waste;
I have asked my Guru
And he has convinced me
There is no other place but God.

Though thy floor be a mosaic of diamond and ruby,
And there be on the floor a couch, adorned with blood-red stones.
And though on the couch there reclineth
A maiden bedecked with jewels,
Her limbs aflame with passion,
Even so, Man, beware, lest thou forget
And remember not the Name of God.

Though thou art adept in *Siddhis*,
Endowed with occult powers,
And powers to acquire wealth;
Though thou canst change thy shape,
At will be seen or unseen;
Though men revere and adore thee,
Even so, Man, beware, lest thou forget
And remember not the Name of God.
Though higher than kings among men, thou art Emperor,
Seated on the imperial throne,

Warded by disciplined armies;
Though thy writ run the wide world over,
Nānak, it passeth like the wind,
Beware, Man, lest thou forget
And remember not the Name of God.

Sri Rag, page 14

2

kot kotī merī ārjā pavan pīan apīāo

Were my span of life to extend to a million years,
And if I could live upon the air alone,
Never assailed by sleep, in a deep dark cave
Where neither the light of the sun nor the light of the moon,
Could pierce down to distract me,
Even so my God, I could not know Thy price,
Nor say how great is Thy Name;
True is the Formless One and Self-Existent,
On hearing the Word, one utters the Word;
If the Lord wills, then one has longing for Him.

Were I slashed to shreds and ground into pulp,
Wasted by fires and reduced to ashes,
Even so my God, I could not know Thy price,
Nor say how great is Thy Name.

Were I to hover like a bird soaring
Through skies innumerable,
And vanish beyond the range of mortal vision,
Self-sustained, not needing food or drink
Even so, my God, I could not know Thy price,
Nor say how great is Thy Name.

Had I studied unmeasured loads of books,
And become the master-scholar of their lore,
And had I a pen to write with the speed of the wind,
A pen filled with inexhaustible ink,
Even so my God, I could not know Thy price,
Nor say how great is Thy Name.

Sri Rag, page 14

3

ik til pyārā vīsarai rog vādā man māhi

This is the greatest sickness of the soul,
To forget even for a second, the Beloved.
There is no comfort hereafter
For him whose heart is empty of God.
Through the grace of the Guru
The tired soul has refreshment;
The praise of God banishes inner desire.
Day and night O anxious heart of mine,
Say and repeat: Praise be to God.
But that man is rare indeed
Who never forgets the Name of God.

When the light of the soul blends with the Universal Light,
And the human mind commingles
With the Mind of all things,
Then our petty being,
With its violence, doubt and sorrow disappears.
Through the grace of the Guru
Such spiritual union taketh place
Blessed are they in whose hearts resideth the Lord.

Let that man be in love with the body,
And make the body his spouse
Who would fain live the life of the senses.
Love not that which endures not.
The Lord is the Spouse who on His couch
Enjoyeth the love of the Righteous.

The Guru thus having taught you,
Disciples: quench in the water
Of the Lord's Name the four fires,
Cruelty, anger, greed and worldly love;
Then the lotus of the inner heart shall blossom;
Then the thirst of the soul shall be quenched with nectar.
Nānak, make the true Guru thy friend;
Then in the court of the Lord thou shalt be happy.

Sri Rag, page 21

4
amal kar dhartī bīj sabdo

O my foolish friend,
Know thus thy Hell and Heaven:
Thy deeds are the soil, the Guru's words the seed,
The Divine Truth is the water
Whose runnels make fertile the fields.
The farmer who thus farms his fields
Will reap the fruits of Faith.
But know well, mere talk wins no profit;
The pride of earthly riches
And the delusion that is born
From the love of created forms,
These waste human life.

The mind, like a frog,
Wallows in the evil mud of the senses
And knows not that the lotus flower
Springs from the same pond;
That the Guru is like the honey bee,
Buzzing around it,
Daily reminding the frog of the lotus
Through his Word.
But how can they know
Whom the Lord hath not made aware.

All advice addressed to a mind,
Sunk in sensuality
Is so much waste of labour;
Those on whom descends the grace of God
Are His favourites;
They keep the Lord ever in their hearts.

Though thou keepest the thirty fasts,
Though thou sayest the five prayers daily with the congregation,
Beware, Beware, lest the evil One turn them all to naught.
Saith Nānak: Truly would you tread
Upon the path of life.
Why then, do you gather worldly goods.

Sri Rag, pages 23, 24

5

tū daryāo dānā bīnā mai machlī kaise ant lahañ

Lord, Thou mighty River, all-knowing, all-seeing,
And I like a little fish in Thy great waters,
How shall I sound Thy depths?
How shall I reach Thy shores?
Wherever I go, I see Thee only,
And snatched out of Thy Waters I die of separation.
I know not the fisher,
I see not the net
But flapping in my agony I call upon Thee for help.

O Lord who pervadeth all things,
In my folly I thought Thou wert far,
But no deed I do can ever be out of Thy sight;
Thou who art All-seeing, all things Thou seest:
I am not worthy to serve Thee,
Nor do I glory in Thy Name.

Thy gifts are my portion,
There is no other door
To which I may go;
This then is the humble prayer
Of Thy servant, Nānak:
Accept my mind and my body
As devoted unto Thee.

The Lord is near, the Lord is distant,
The Lord is in the mean between these two extremes;
He watcheth His creation,
He hears His creation, for He is the Creator;
Nānak, whatever the Lord wills,
That cometh to pass.

Sri Rag, page 25

6
machlī jāl nā jāniā sar khārā asgāh

Vast and without bounds are the waters of the Ocean,
In them a fish swam
And did not spy the net;
It was very beautiful and clever:
Why then was it so unsuspecting?
Through its own acts the bait caught it,
And the moment of destiny cannot be changed.

Brethren hearken unto me,
And through this parable
Learn how Death taketh man.
As the fish in the story, so is mortal man.
The fatal net is flung without a warning:
All, all are within the sway of death;
Only the Guru may check Death's onslaught;

Truth makes us free, Truth destroys doubt,
Truth destroys every sickness of the soul.
May I be as a sacrifice unto those
Who have been judged true in the Lord's Presence.

As the small birds of the air are helpless
Against the hawk swooping down from the skies,
And against the nets of the hunter below
Even so with mortal man.
Those whom the Guru protects escape in safety,
The rest are caught by the bait.
Without the protection of the Holy Name
One by one we are weeded out
And cast away
Comradeless, friendless.

True eternally and acclaimed to be true
Is the Lord, True is His Realm:
His Truth resides in the hearts of those
Who believe thus in His Truth.
Those who have attained the Guru's wisdom
Are pure in heart and speech.

Pray to the Lord, to the True Guide,
That in Him thou mayest meet the Beloved Friend.
In this meeting the soul is happy
And Death dies of its own disease.
May I live in the Name,
May the Name in me be indwelling.

Without the Guru to teach us, we walk in darkness,
Without the Word, we have no understanding.
The Word of the Guru is light,
His Word's light leads to the Truth.
There, Death has no existence.
His light is joined with Light.

Thou art our companion, Thou art Wise,
Thou blessest people with union
Through the Guru's teaching,
Exalted by Thy Name, O Unbounded Being.
That to which the immortal Word of the Guru
Beareth eternal witness
Is the Abode of Immortality.

By His Will, all is created,
Through His Will, all life pulsates;
Under His Will, Death has dominion
Over all creation and all life.
By His Will also the blessed abide
In His Eternal Truth;
All-Pervasive, Omnipotent, is His Will.
Such, O Nānak, is the helplessness of Man.

Sri Rag, page 55

7

ro man aisī har sion prīt kar

Listen My heart!
Let thy love be that of the lotus for the pool,
Though the ripples shake the lotus and torment it,
It flowereth and loveth even more the waters.
Let thy love be that of the fish for the water
Without which they perish.

O my heart how shalt thou find freedom
Except thou find it through love;
In the hearts of His saints
God indwelleth,
To them He giveth the treasure of true devotion.

Listen, my heart: love God ceaselessly
As the fish loveth water:
The deeper the water
The happier and more tranquil the fish.
God alone knoweth the suffering
Of fish separated from the waters.

O my heart, listen:
Love God even as the Chatrik bird loveth the raindrops.
Rivers in spate and the drenched uplands
Are of no avail to the Chatrik;
Nothing but the raindrops can quench its thirst.
As a man sows, so shall he reap
That which the Lord ordaineth must come to pass.

O my heart, listen:
Love God as water loves milk.
The water must suffer, must evaporate
Before the heat can touch the milk.
God is the Separator, God is the Joiner:
The Lord is He that exalteth through Truth.

O my heart listen:
Love God as the Sheldrake in the fable loveth the sun;
It sleepeth not for a moment:
At night when it cannot see,
It considers the Beloved, who is close to be far.
The self-willed are involved in calculations,
But what the Lord ordaineth cometh to pass.
And howsoever hard a man endeavoureth,
Who can tell of His Bounds?
Only through the Guru's teaching is this revealed;
In Truth alone is our peace.

Those who encounter the Guru
Achieve an indestructible love of God.
The Guru bestows Divine Knowledge
And unveils the mysteries of the three worlds.
That man whose feet are set
On the path of virtue
Never abandoneth the pure Name.

Gone are those free birds of the air,
Who had their nurture on the happy plains;
How transient is life?
All its sport but the fleeting joy of a moment.
Who is ever successful,
Who wins any game
Except by the Will of God?

Without the Guru's help we cannot burn
To nothingness the ashes of self-love;
For the Guru kindles in the human hearts
The fire of the love of God.
Through the Guru's Word alone
There comes the moment of knowing:
'My Self is that Self.'
Through faith in the Guru the True Self is known.
What else do we need to know?

The self is ever one with the Self:
This certainty is obtained through the Guru's Word.
But those who are tied to their small selves
Shall not know this,
And separation and frustration is their lot.
Nānak, God is the one Way
God is the one Goal;
There is no other refuge.

Sri Rag, page 59

8

rām nām man bedhia avar kiā karī vicār

My mind is pierced with the Name of God;
What else remains to hold my mind?
In the contemplation of the Word is bliss,
In the absorption of God is joy.
The name of the Lord is as my pillar;
Lord, may Thy will prevail.

O my heart!
The Will of God is ever just and true.
Give thy love, O heart, to Him;
Who hath created the mind and the body,
And who hath adorned them.
Slice thy body shred by shred,
Burn it as incense on the priestly altars,
Burn thy bones and thy brain
As faggots in the fire.
Such austerities, even though they were innumerable,
Are as nothing compared with the contemplation of God.

Have thy body sawn in two:
Have thy head severed from thy body;
Have thy body rotting in perpetual snows;
Even the acceptance of such penance
Cannot wash the mind clean of its evils.
Such penances are nothing as compared with the contemplation of God.
This have I found by test and trial.
Give in alms golden mansions,
Give scores of elephants, give high-mettled steeds,
Give herds of cattle, give pasture-lands;
Yet the sin of pride hath not departed
From the innermost courts of thy hearts;
These are the true alms my Guru hath given me:
A mind that is pierced with the Name of God.

There are many dogmas, there are many systems,
There are many scriptural revelations,
Many modes to fetter the mind:
But the saint seeks for release through Truth;
Truth is higher than all these, and higher
Still is the life lived in Truth.
All that is, is great and high:
There is nothing base.
One potter hath fashioned all the pots,
One Light pervadeth all Creation.
Through Grace is the Truth revealed,
And none can resist Grace.

In the company of the holy congregation,
We attain to the Guru:
The love of the Guru and his peace are awakened in the mind,
We grasp the ineffable story of the Lord,
If the spirit of the True Guru is within us.
The soul then drinks nectar and feels peace;
And honour is attained in the Presence of the Lord.

Divine Music is heard
In every soul reverberant,
Continuous, self-sustained, a revelation!
Few are the Saints
Who are granted this understanding:
Nānak, release from bondage
Comes from contemplating the Word,
Forget not the Holy Name.

Sri Rag, page 62

9

phakar jātī phakar nau

Noble birth and great fame,
Are as worthless as dust:
God is the only protecting shade;
A man may boast to men of his own goodness,
But the truth about him will be known in God's presence;
He whom the Lord exalteth, is exalted indeed.

Sri Rag ki Var, page 83

10

kabudh dūmnī kūd kasāyan

Perversity of the soul is like a woman of low caste,
Lack of compassion like a butcher woman;
The desire to find fault with others
Is like a scavenger woman,
The sin of wrath is like an utter outcast;
What use is it to draw a line around your kitchen[1].
If four such vices keep you company.

Make your discipline the practice of truth,
Make the square you draw round your kitchen
The practice of virtue;
Make the ceremonial cleansing of your body
The meditation of Holy Name.
Saith Nānak: Those alone shall be deemed good and pure
That walk not in the way of sin.

Sri Rag ki Var, page 91

11

kuḍ bol murdār khāe

Nānak: such are the blasphemers,
Who set themselves up
As the leaders of the world;
They consume daily the forbidden fruit of falsehood,
And yet they preach to others
What is right and what is wrong.
Themselves deluded, they delude those also
Who follow them in their path.

Rag Majh ki Var, page 140

---

[1] Hindus of extreme orthodoxy draw a line round their kitchen, and if anybody crosses that line, the food is polluted. Guru Nanak points out that food is not polluted by the presence of other people near it but by the evil passions and habits within us. What use will the outward and ceremonial purity of the cooking square be, when we are impure within? The four evils are compared with four women of low caste.

12

je rat lagai kapḍai jāmā hoe palīt

If one smear of blood pollutes a garment
And renders it unclean, to be worn at prayer;
How can they that like vampires suck human blood pass as pure;
Nānak, before the Name of God is uttered by the tongue
Let the heart first be cleansed;
All other outward appearances of piety are worthless.

Rag Majh ki Var, page 140

13

mehar masīt sidak musala hak halāl korān

Let compassion be thy mosque,
Let faith be thy prayer mat,
Let honest living be thy Korān,
Let modesty be the rules of observance,
Let piety be the fasts thou keepest;
In such wise strive to become a Moslem:
Right conduct the Ka'ba; Truth the Prophet,
Good deeds thy prayer;
Submission to the Lord's Will thy rosary;
Nānak, if this thou do, the Lord will be thy Protector.

Rag Majh ki Var, page 140

14

panj nivājāṅ vakht panj

Five prayers, five times a day,
With five different names;
Make the first prayer, truth;
The second to lawfully earn your daily bread;
The third: charity in the Name of God,
Fourth: purity of the mind,
Fifth: the adoration of God.

Practise these five virtues,
And let good deeds be your article of faith: the Kalmā;
Then you can call yourself truly a Moslem.
By the practice of hypocrisy, Nānak,
A man is deemed false through and through.

Rag Majh ki Var, page 141

15

je dehai dukh lāīai pāp gareh do rāh

Though my body be crippled with disease,
Though the relentless stars bring endless misfortune on me,
Though bloody tyrants fill my soul with terror,
Though all these miseries be at once heaped on my head,
Even then, my Lord, I shall praise Thee:
And I shall not grow weary of exalting Thy Holy Name.

Rag Majh ki Var, page 142

16

kiā khādai kiā paidhai hoe

What is the use of rich food and fine clothes,
When the Truth does not dwell within us?
What is the use of fresh fruit, of sugar, of butter,
Of flour and meat in abundance,
Of splendid raiments, and of soft beds,
And a life of sensual delight?
What use to a king his armies, his wise ministers and his brave commanders,
If in his heart he has not the Divine Name.
Nānak, all these things are as dust.

Rag Majh ki Var, page 142

17

machī tārū kiā kare paṅkhī kiā akāṣ

The fact that the skies are without limit
Bothers not the bird;
The depths of water bother not the fish;
A stone is not sensitive to freezing cold;
What do the pleasures of married life
Matter to an eunuch?
If you smear a dog with sandal paste
It will not change its nature.
Reading of scriptures to the deaf
Is of no avail.
Offer a cow gold
And it will prefer to munch hay;
Can a blind man see
Surrounded by a blaze of fifty lamps?
Steel beaten for ever will not become as soft as cotton;
Nānak, such is the nature of the fool,
Who always talketh foolishly.

Rag Majh ki Var, page 143

18

kaiṅhāṅ kañcan tute sār

If bronze or iron or gold breaks
The smith weldeth it with fire;
When love is broken between man and wife
The birth of a child knits it up.
When the king demandeth a token of loyalty
And the good subject payeth his taxes,
There is a bond between the subject and the king.

When a hungry man is given food
He reneweth his bond with the world.
In times of drought and famine,
Heavy rains and the flooding of rivers
Retie a broken knot.

To deepen the ties of love
Tender speech is the linkage.
If anyone speaketh and practiseth Truth·
He is linked to the Scriptures;
And the dead are tied to the living
Through their past virtuous deeds.
These are the ties, the links, the knots of the world.

But the only way to deal with a fool
Is to smite him on the face
When he uttereth his folly.
And between Man and God
The way to establish a tie
Is through the praise of the Lord;
Nānak, having pondered, saith this.

Rag Majh ki Var, page 143

19

ham zer zamin dunyā pīrā masāyakā rāyā

The grave lies at the end of the road for all living things:
For the Master and his disciples,
For the prophets and for the kings;
The greatest of the earth
Are creatures of the moment that passeth;
Thou alone art! Thou alone art!

Rag Majh ki Var, page 143

20

nā dev dānvā narā

Neither gods nor demigods nor men endure,
The adepts in mystery, those with magical powers,
Are all creaturely, are all mortal.
It is only God that endureth.
Thou alone art! Thou alone art!

Rag Majh ki Var, page 143

21

nā dāde dahind ādmī

The final vision of justice is not with Man,
Nor with any creature in the Universe.
The Lord's alone is the vision of Justice;
Thou alone art! Thou alone art!

Rag Majh ki Var, page 144

22

nā sūr sas mandalo

Neither the lunar nor the solar spheres,
Nor the dry land nor the waters over the earth
Nor the air nor the moving winds in the limitless spaces
Shall endure ever;
Thou alone art! Thou alone art!

Rag Majh ki Var, page 144

23

nā rijk dast ā kase

It is in no one's power to give livelihood to another,
The Lord alone is the Sustainer of all,
The One endureth, naught else is enduring;
Thou alone art! Thou alone art!

Rag Majh ki Var, page 144

24

parindae nā girāh jar

Behold the birds of the air,
They build themselves no granaries;
They construct no tanks of water,

They depend on the forest trees,
And on the natural pools.
The Lord provideth them all.
Thou alone art! Thou alone art!

25

kal kātī rāje kasāī dharam paṅkh kar udariā

This age is like a drawn Sword, the kings are butchers;
Goodness hath taken wings and flown.
In the dark night of falsehood,
I espy not the moon of Truth anywhere;
I grope after Truth and am bewildered.

I see no path in the darkness;
It is the obstinacy with which Man
Clings to his petty self-hood
That causeth this anguish;
Nānak asketh: where is the path of salvation.

Rag Majh ki Var, page 145

26

hauṅ dhādhī vekār kāre lāyā

I was a minstrel out of work;
The Lord gave me employment.
The Mighty One instructed me:
Night and day, sing my praise!
The Lord did summon this minstrel
To his High Court;
On me He bestowed the robe of honour
Of those who exalt Him.

On me He bestowed the Nectar in a Cup,
The Nectar of His True and Holy Name.
Those who at the bidding of the Guru
Feast and take their fill
Of the Lord's Holiness
Attain peace and joy.

Thy minstrel spreadeth Thy glory
By singing Thy Word;
Nānak, through adoring the Truth
We attain to the All-Highest.

Rag Majh ki Var, page 150

27

dar ghar ghari dar dari daru jāe

Entertain in the heart the fear of the Lord;
Through the fear of the Lord, all other fears are conquered.
Of what merit is any fear
That leadeth not to fearlessness
But to other and worse fears?
There is no other place of sanctuary, O Lord, but Thyself;
Nothing can come to pass but what Thou ordaineth;
What fear should we then have except the fear of the Lord.
All other fears are but phantoms
Of the mind, too much attached to the worldly things.

Man in himself hath no self-dwelling power
Either to live or die, to swim or drown.
All things are as the Creator ordaineth.
Birth and death are both by His Will;
His Will is supremely sovereign, heretofore and hereafter.

Violence, worldly love, greed and pride
Are insatiate like a restless river.
Unless the fear of God is thy food and drink,
Unless the fear of God is thy whole sustenance,
Degradation and death are thy lot, O Man.

He who putteth his trust in mortal man
Putteth his trust in mortality;
God is our last stay and our final help,
There is naught that He is not Lord of.
Nānak, His ways are hard indeed to expound.

Rag Gauri Guareri, page 151

28

avar panc ham ek janā

The flesh hath five weaknesses,
How single, and without help,
Shall I guard my House and my goods against them?
They are forever besieging me,
They break in when they can.
On whom shall I call for help?
Poor pitiful heart, repeat the Name of God;
Terrible, indeed, are the pangs of death that assail thee.

This God-built house of the body,
Of which the soul is a tenant, has many doors.
The five temptations that flesh is the heir to
Make daily raids upon it,
Whilst the soul disports itself in the delights of the senses
Thinking the house lent for a season
Shall last even for ever.

Death demolishes the house, removes from it
The indwelling life, and takes into custody
The soul, the house's tenant:
Certainly the soul is solitary and lonely;
Death like a bludgeon, strikes him on the head
Who walked proudly, his neck arrayed in plumes,
Whose bride craved for ornaments of gold and silver,
Whose friends craved from his feasts, much food and drink.
Nānak, the man who commits sins for such trifles
Is bound hand and foot.

Rag Gauri Cheti, page 155

29

rain gavāī soe ke divas gavāyā khāe

I have lost my nights in sleep,
I have lost my days in pursuit of sensual pleasures.
Oh, how cheaply we sell
This precious human life.

Fool, thou hast forgotten God;
Thou wilt have to repent hereafter.
Even on the morrow, utter shall be thy despair.
On earth man sets no bounds
To his heaping up of wealth
But doth not desire the Lord, the truly Boundless;
Verily, they lose the Lord, who gain this world.

And if wishes were wealth, beggars would be millionaires:
Not by wishes but by deeds
Is the last goal reached.
Nānak, the Creator watcheth over His creation;
The Lord's is the last Judgement:
But the how and the why of it no mortal knoweth.

Rag Gauri Bairagan, page 156

30

dudh bin dhen pankh bin pankhī

A cow is no use without milk,
Nor a bird without wings;
Vegetation withers without water,
A king without subjects is a hollow sham.
Those in whom the eyes of the spirit
Have not been opened
Are nothing without Thy Name.
In forgetting Thee, there is much sorrow.
Spare me that sorrow, O Lord,
May I never forget Thee.

Dim is the light of my eyes,
My tongue moveth but feebly,
My ears have lost their hearing:
My legs cannot move without a crutch.
This is what becomes of human life
When we do not serve God.

In thy heart's garden plant,
Like seeds, the Word of the Guru
And water thy garden with love:

And all thy orchards shall bear the precious fruitage
Of the Holy Name of God?
But oh poor helpless Man:
What can he ever achieve without God's grace?

All living beings in the world, O Lord, are Thine;
And without Thine aid they wither and then they die;
All the joys and the struggles of life are Thy gifts,
But only by Thy Holy Name is that gift sustained:
To die to the petty self within us,
That, in truth, is everlasting life:
All other life is squandering, is death
Thus sayeth Nānak: May the Lord's Will prevail.

Rag Asa, page 354

31

khurāsān khasmānā kiā hindustān darāyā

Though Khurasan has been shielded by Thee,
Though terror has struck at the heart of Hindustān,
Thou, O Creator of all things,
Takest to Thyself no blame;
Thou hast sent Yama disguised as the great Moghal, Babar.
Terrible was the slaughter,
Loud were the cries of the lamenters.
Did this not awaken pity in Thee, O Lord?

Thou art part and parcel of all things equally, O Creator:
Thou must feel for all men and all nations.
If a strong man attacketh another who is equally strong;
Where is the grief in this, or whose is the grievance?
But when a fierce tiger preys on the helpless cattle,
The Herdsman must answer for it.

A Kingdom that was a Jewel
Was wasted by the dogs,
No one will mourn their passing.
Praise, praise be to God
Who bringeth the people together and divideth them also.

The man who thinks himself great,
And enjoys himself to the height of his heart's desire,
In the Lord's eyes is no more than an insect
Nibbling an ear of corn.
The true profit of life is learning to die
And repeating His Name, saith Nānak.

Rag Asa, page 360

32

jin sir sohan paṭīāṅ māṅgīh pāe sandhūr

The tresses that adorned these lovely heads,
And were parted with vermilion,
Have been shorn with cruel shears:
Dust has been thrown on their shaven heads.
They lived in ease in palaces,
Now they must beg by the roadside,
Having no place for their shelter.
Glory unto Thee, O Lord of Glory,
Who can understand Thy ways, O God?
Surely Thy ways are strange and Thy dispensation!

When these whose heads are shorn were married,
Fair indeed seemed their bridegrooms beside them.
They were brought home in palanquins carved with ivory.
Pitchers of water were waved over their heads
In ceremonial welcome.
Ornate fans glittered waving above them.

At the first entry into the new home,
Each bride was offered a gift of a lakh of rupees;
Another lakh when each stood up to take her post in her new home;
Coconut shreddings and raisins were among the delicious fruits,
Served to them at their tables.
These beauties lent charm to the couches they reclined on.
Now they are dragged away, with ropes round their necks;
Their necklaces are snapped and their pearls scattered.

Their beauty and wealth were once their greatest assets,
Their beauty and wealth are their greatest enemies now;
Barbarous soldiers have taken them prisoners and disgraced them.
God casts down, God exalteth, whomsoever He will.

If these folk had taken heed to the future,
Need they have been reduced to such plight?
Pursuing worldly love and sensual pleasure,
The princes of Hindustān have lost their heads.
Desecration and desolation follow in the footsteps
Of the Great Moghal, Babar.
None, none in Hindustān can eat his supper in peace.

For the Muslim woman the hour of prayer is past,
For the Hindu, the time of worship is gone;
How can they that were proud of their caste,
And punctilious in ceremonial performance worship now;
They who never thought of their own *Rama*
Are now denied the name of *Allah*.

Few, some very few,
From this havoc return home,
And others enquire of them
About their lost dear ones;
Many are lost for ever
And weeping and anguish are the lot of those who survive.
Ah, Nānak, how completely helpless mere men are.
It is God's Will that is done, for ever and ever.

Rag Asa, page 417

33

SELECTIONS:
'PATTI: ACROSTIC ON PUNJABI ALPHABET'

(i)

chachai chāyā vartī sabh antar

Ignorance pervadeth all creatures,
By Thine own ordaining, O Lord.
Doubt and delusion prevail:
Thy creatures suffer from ignorance
Of the true nature of Self-hood.
But through Thy grace, also they meet the Guru
Through whom ignorance is removed.

(ii)

papai pātṣāh parmeṣvar vekhan ko parpanc kīā

The Lord God is King.
For His own delight He created all the worlds.
He seeth, He knoweth, He comprehendeth all things.
From within and without,
There is naught that He doth not pervade.

Rag Asa Patti, 10, 24, page 433

34

tū sun harnā kāliā kī vāḍīai rātā rām

O black buck, listen to me!
Why dost thou crave to break into the fenced-off fields?
The delight of cropping forbidden herbage
Lasteth but for a few days.
Thereafter there is sorrow in store.
Sorrow is the wages of sin
On which thou art intent.
Those who forsake God's Name
Suffer in the flames of evil;

Delight of the senses lasts no longer
Than a surface ripple on water,
Than the lightning's sudden flash.

Black deer, O my Soul, thou forgettest the Lord,
There is no peace except in the Lord,
Forsake Him not!
O black deer, O heart of a fool,
Hold on to the Lord:
Nānak warneth thee, by the other road
There lieth but death, but destruction.

O my soul, thou honey-bee,
Buzzing around the blossoms to rifle their sweets,
Hear me, thy sorrow is great:
I asked the Guru in so many words
'What is the true path?'
And the Guru in so many words answered me:
O honey bee thou art lost in worldly flowers,
When the sun rises after death,
Thy soul will suffer as body scalded by oil.

Without the Word of the Guru
Man is stupid and cannot find his way,
He dieth and forever suffereth agony.
Forget not God, O heart of a fool, O honey bee:
On the other road lieth death,
On the other road lieth destruction, saith Nānak.

My soul thou art not a native of this world,
Wherefore then get caught in the net?
Entertain within thyself the Holy Name of God.
The fish like the human soul is ensnared in the net of death,
It weeps and gasps in agony,
And now she knows that life ever pleasant was a delusion.
Adore and cherish the Lord
And cast out baseless fears.
Pay heed, O my soul, to this admonition of Nānak:
My soul, that art not native to this place,
In thine inner depths cherish the true Lord.

As streaming rivers that start from the same source
Are separated but meet in the Ocean,
So do souls meet in the Infinite,
One in a million knows
That age upon age
The world's illusions enchant and poison the soul.
Those that contemplate the Guru
Learn easily and realize God.

Those who do not cherish the Lord's Name
Wander, deceived and bewildered;
Without such cherishing of the Lord's Name,
Without the love of His Eternal Being,
Man can have no destiny except remorse and anguish.
Nānak utters a truth:
Through the Word of the Guru
The long estrangement of the soul and God end in meeting.

Rag Asa, page 438

35

SELECTIONS FROM ĀSĀ-DĪ-VĀR

(1)

balihārī gur apne diohādī sadvār

Countless times a day,
Hail, unto the Guru all hail.
Whose transmuting spirit has changed
Mortals into god-like saints.

(2)

paḍ paḍ gaḍī ladīai

One may read cartloads of books,
With caravan-loads of books to follow;
One may study shiploads of volumes,
And heap them pile on pile in his cellars;

One may read for years and on years,
And spend every month of the year in reading only;
And thus read all ones life,
Right up to his last breath.
Of all things, contemplative life
Is really what matters;
All else is the fret and fever of the egoistic minds.

(3)

paḍiā hovai gunehgār

A scholar who sins will not be spared,
An unlettered saint will not be entrapped,
A man will by his actions and deeds,
Be judged and known good or bad;
Play not the game of life in such a way,
That you may be denied a place in His Presence.
The scholar as well as the unlettered man
By their deeds will be judged in His Court.
The self-willed and the boastful
Will suffer agonizing blows.

(4)

dayā kapāh santokh sūt

Out of the cotton of compassion,
Spin the thread of contentment,
Tie the knot of continence,
Give it the twist of virtues;
Make such a sacred thread
O Pundit for your inner self.

Such a thread will not break,
Nor get soiled, be burnt, be lost.
Blessed is the man, O Nānak,
Who makes it part of his life.
This cotton thread, for a penny you buy
Sitting in a square, mud plastered,
You put it around the necks of others.

In the ears some words you whisper, O Brahmin,
And claim to be a spiritual teacher.
With the death of the wearer falls the thread,
Thus without the thread he departs from the earth.

(5)

bhand jamīai bhand nimīai

Of a woman are we conceived,
Of a woman we are born,
To a woman are we betrothed and married,
It is a woman who is friend and partner of life,
It is woman who keeps the race going,
Another companion is sought when the life-partner dies,
Through woman are established social ties.
Why should we consider woman cursed and condemned
When from woman are born leaders and rulers.
From woman alone is born a woman,
Without woman there can be no human birth.
Without woman, O Nānak, only the True One exists.
Be it men or be it women,
Only those who sing His glory
Are blessed and radiant with His Beauty,
In His Presence and with His grace
They appear with a radiant face.

Rag Asa, pages 463-75

36

morīn run jhun lāiā bhaine sāvan āyā

Listen, my sisters, to the sound of the rain coming down the water-spouts,
And to the exulting cry of the peacocks:
It is the rainy month of Sāvan,
O Beloved, Thy glance pierces my heart
Like the point of a sharp dagger;
It bound and bewitched me.

For one glimpse of Thee I make myself a sacrifice:
Glory to Thy Holy Name!
When Thou choosest to dwell in my heart
Honour is mine, I am exalted.
When Thou forgettest me, I am as one abandoned.

O woman, smash thy bracelets by thy bed-side,
With the bangles break thy arms,
What use this ornamentation,
When the Lord the lover is with another.
Not the vendor of the bangles,
Nor the bangles themselves,
Are such as would appeal to Him.
Arms that have not embraced the Lord
Burn in anguish.

All my friends have gone to their lovers,
I wretched, left alone,
Whither shall I go.
Friends, I am comely
But I please not the Lord.
I took pains to plait my hair,
Put vermilion in the parting,
But when I went to my tryst
I was utterly wretched.

I wept and the world wept with me,
The birds of the forests also wept,
But my soul in separation wept not.
In my dream He came and went away.
I wept copious tears,
I cannot come to Thee, O Lord
Nor send anyone to plead for me.
Blessed sleep revisit my couch once more,
It may be in my dream I shall see Him again.
Nānak, what offering shall I make to the messenger
Who will bring me a message from God my lover.
I shall cut my head and make a seat thereof,
And be attendance on him,
Why not die and be a sacrifice
When the Lord has forsaken thee?

Rag Vadhans, pages 557–8

37

jālo aisī rīt jit mai pyarā visrai

Give up the ways that turn thee from God,
Nānak, only that love is real
Which leadeth men to the Lord.

Rag Vadhans, Var, page 565

38

man halī kirsānī karnī sarm pānī tan khet

THESE ARE THE SECRETS OF TRUE HUSBANDRY,
The body is the field; let mind be the ploughman,
Good deeds thy ploughing,
Let thine honest strivings be the runnels
That irrigate the field.
Sow the seed of the Holy Name.
Make the clods of the field level with contentment;
Wear, as a farmer, the peasant garb of humility.
Then with the grace of God, His love will blossom.
Blessed is the peasant who farms in this wise.
And thou, great man, thy worldly goods will not go with thee;
Maya, the veil of illusion hath misled the world
And few indeed know this to be so.

These are the secrets of honest shop-keeping:
Our transient life is our shop,
And the Holy Name is the merchandise
With which we are entrusted;
Alertness of mind and purity of deed
Are the warehouses in which to store the Name.
Let thy dealings be with the saints;
They are sound, reliable customers.
Take a fair profit and be happy.

Travelling tradesman, let thy trade be in scripture;
And let thy wagon be drawn by the horses of Truth.
Gather good deeds for travelling expenses
And tarry not in thy way.

When thou reachest thy goal and tradest in God's country, heaven,
After thy travels thou shalt enjoy thy peace.

Man set in authority,
Let devotion to God be thy service,
Let thy toil be faith in the Name.
Check thy mind from wandering after temptation;
Stand alert on guard against all evil,
So from all men thou shalt earn the praise,
And the Lord, thy Kind, will delight in thee
With a fourfold increase of His Love.

Rag Sorath, page 595

39

jaisī mai āvai khasm kī bānī

As the word of the Lord descendeth upon me,
So I make it known friend Lallo;
With evil as his best man,
Bringing a crowd of sins as his bridal procession,
Like a bridegroom Babar hath hasted from Kabul,
To seize by force as his bride, O Lallo,
The wealth of Hindustān.
Modesty and righteousness have both vanished away,
Falsehood leading the van, holds the field, O Lallo;
Both the Qazi and the Brahmin are out of work;
The devil reads the marriage services.
Muslim women who read the Korān
In their agony will cry on God, O Lallo;
Hindu women of high caste or low caste
Will meet with the same dire fate.
Men will sing hymns in praise of murder, O Nānak;
And instead of saffron smear themselves with blood.

Though this is a city of corpses, Nānak exalteth the Lord in it,
And uttereth this true saying:
The Lord who made men, gave them their different stations:
He sitteth aloof from their doings and watcheth them all.

Just and true is the Lord; just and true is His Judgement.
Just and true is the Judgement He meteth out
As a warning to us all.

Bodies of men shall be rent like the shreds of cloth;
And let Hindustān remember what I now say:
The arrival of the Moghals shall be in '78,
Their departure in '97.
And then again shall arise the disciple of a Hero.
Nānak hath spoken the word of the true Lord now
And will proclaim the truth
At the true Lord's appointed hour.

Rag Tilang, page 722

40

sāgar main būnd būnd mai sāgar

The drop of water is in the sea,
And the sea is in the drop of water;
Who shall solve this riddle?
Who knoweth the secret?
He from whom all creation came,
He who surveyeth that which He hath created,
He, the Lord, is the One knower of the secret;
And the man who understandeth this in his heart
Is freed from human bondage,
Is made at one with the Lord.

Here is another riddle!
At noon there can be sheer darkness of midnight,
At midnight there can be the blaze of the noonday sun;
At the centre of burning heat there can be freezing cold;
This is the riddle of life:
We could not have solved it without the Guru's guidance,
No one else knows the answer, however astute.

Master of Divine knowledge read me this riddle:
Man is born of woman and woman of man!
The Word leads to concentration,
Concentration to knowledge,
That is the miraculous tale of the Guru's Word.

The Eternal Light indwells in the human mind,
And the human mind is the emanation of that Light,
And our five senses are the Light's disciples.
Nānak, may I be a sacrifice
To those who cherish the unique Word of the Guru.

Rag Ramkali, page 878

41

Dakhnī Oṁkār

(i)

lāj marantī mar gaī

All shyness and hesitation has died away,
The veil of separation I have cast away;
My mother-in-law is no more there
To create doubt and delusion
And stand between me and my love.
My Beloved has sent for me to a love tryst,
In my heart is the joy of His Song;
In the embrace of the Beloved,
I feel lost in Him,
All doubts and delusions have departed
And the light shines within.

(ii)

kām krodh kāyan ko gāle

Lust and wrath waste the body,
As borax melts the gold.
But the gold that can stand the test of fire
Is valued highly by the goldsmith,
So it is with the souls.
Man is an animal,
And egoism is the butcher.
In the hands of the Creator
Is the saving grace.

Rag Ramkali, page 931

42

Sidh-Gosht

CHARPAT YOGI QUESTIONS

dunyā sāgar dutar kahīai

The sea of life is hard to cross,
How can we safely reach the other shore?

NĀNAK ANSWERS

āpe akhai āpe samjhai

Thou hast stated the problem correctly,
What answer then, need I give thee?
As the lotus flower
Does not drown in the pool,
As the duck
Is not made wet by the pond.
As the flower thrusts upwards,
As the duck swims,
So with the mind intent
Upon the Word of the Guru
One can safely cross
The great sea of life,
Repeating the Holy Name,
Living in an aloneness
Utterly intent,
Upon the Alone.
In a life of worldly hopes,
Purging the mind
Of worldly desires.
Nanak is the slave
Of the one who graspeth
The ungraspable
And maketh others grasp Him.

LOHARIPA YOGI PLEADS

hāti bātī rahai nirāle

Know this the way of Yoga:
Shun towns and highways,
Live in the forests under the trees,
On roots and wild fruit.
The Yogis must live
The contemplative life;
Also for purification
One must visit
The places of pilgrimages.

NĀNAK ANSWERS TO LOHARIPA

hātī bātī nind nā āvai

Even while living
In towns and near highways,
Remain alert. Do not covet
Any of the neighbour's goods.
Without the Divine Name
We cannot attain inner peace
Nor still our inner hunger.
As the Guru has shown
The real life of the city
The real life of its shops
Is a life within us.
We must be traders in truth,
We should eat but little,
We should sleep but little,
This, saith Nānak, is the core
Of the idea of Yoga.

LOHARIPA EXPOSTULATES

darṣan bhekh karo jogindrā

But Yoga is a system
Which I beg theè to adopt,
Its symbols are patched coat,
Earings, a beggar's wallet.

Out of the six systems,
Adopt this system of Yoga,
Out of the twelve Yogi sects,
Enter ours, the leading one.
Though thou sayest, only those
Whom God hath enlightened
Have truly grasped God
Control thy mind by my rules
And thou canst attain Yoga.

NĀNAK ANSWERS

antar sabad nirantar mudrā

My own system is constant,
Contemplation of the Word.
My way of wearing earings:
To discard pride and attachment,
My patched coat and beggar's wallet:
Are seeing God in all things.
Only God can make me free.
The Lord is the Truth,
Truth is His Name, says the Guru,
He who will may test this.

A YOGI QUESTIONS

kis karan greh tajio udāsī

Why hast thou left thy home,
Why wanderest thou like an hermit?
In what is thy trade?
How settest thou free thy disciples?

NĀNAK ANSWERS

gurmukh khojat bhae udāsī

I left my home to look for a saint;
The desire to see the Lord
Hath made me a hermit.
My trade is in truth,
Through the grace of God
I shall set free my companions.

A YOGI QUESTIONS

kavan mūl kavan mat velā

What is the source of thy knowledge?
To what period belongeth thy system?
Who is thy Guru, and who are thy disciples?
What teaching keepeth thee in detachment?
Tell us all this, my Child?

NĀNAK ANSWERS

pavan arambh satgur mat velā

With the beginning of the breath of life,
My system began also;
Its source is the Wisdom of the true Guru,
The true Guru is the Word,
And the human mind is the disciple.
What keepeth me in my detachment
Is meditating on the Ungraspable One,
Through the One Divine Word
God is made real to us,
And the saints destroy the flames,
Of attachment to the little self.

MORE QUESTIONS BY A YOGI

main ke dant kion khāiai sār

How can steel be chewed with waxen teeth?
What drug can cure the disease of pride?
How shall we dress a snow man in fire?
In what cage can the mind rest in peace?
What is it that is everywhere,
With which every mind should be one?
What object of concentration
Can teach the mind to turn wholly to itself?

NĀNAK ANSWERS

hauṅ hauṅ mai maiṅ vicoṅ khovai

From within, from within,
Make the Self as naught as naught;
Root out all feelings of otherness
And become at one with God.
True the world is as hard as Steel,
For the stubborn and the self-willed in their folly,
But through the might of the Word
This steel can be digested.
Outside thyself and within thyself
Seek only the knowledge of God.
By the blessings of the true Guru
The flames of desires can be destroyed.

Rag Ramkali, pages 938-47,
verses 4, 5, 7, 8, 9, 10, 17, 18, 43, 44, 45, 46.

43

arbad narbad dhundūkārā

Through uncountable ages,
Complete darkness brooded
Over utter vacancy;
There were no worlds, no firmaments.
The Will of the Lord was alone pervasive;
There was neither night nor day, nor sun nor moon
But only God in ceaseless trance.

No air and no water,
No utterance, no source of life,
No beginning or ending, no growth or decay,
No continents, no regions under the earth,
No swelling oceans or winding rivers.

The higher, the middle, the lower planes did not exist,
Eating time did not exist either,
There was neither heaven nor hell,

Since the cycle of birth and death had not begun,
And so there was no upper region of bliss,
No middle region of purgation,
No lowest region of torment.

There were no gods to inhabit the highest heavens,
No Brahma, no Vishnu, no Siva;
There was the One, the Eternal and none besides;
There was neither male nor female
Neither shaping nor begetting,
There was nothing to experience
Either pleasure or pain.

There were no ascetics and no voluptuaries,
No monks and no hermits,
No religious communities of any sort,
No liturgies, no creeds.
There was no one to think of any one,
Except God to think of Himself.
God was His own emanation,
He judged His own worth and rejoiced in His own Beauty.

There were not any Vaishvanites, counting their basil beads,
There were no ritual observances or pious forbearances;
Krishna was not, nor were his milkmaids,
Neither were tantras and mantra Saktis and all their humbug,
Nor was there any flute player.

There were no churches, with their creeds and rites,
There was no maya, the veil of illusion,
That makes dark and defiles;
There were no castes, since there were no births,
There was no predestination to drag us through
The mud of the worldly attachment and death and rebirth
And the worship of too many gods.

There were no living bodies and souls,
There was nothing and no one to accept or deny the truth:
The great Gorakh and Machindera did not exist.

There was no subject for contemplation,
No object of knowledge,
Nothing to trace the genesis of,
Nothing to sit judgement on.

There were no divisions of caste or rank, no sectarian **antagonisms**,
No idols nor temples, nor creeds of particular nations,
There were no clashing forms of prayer and worship,
Nor any to worship or pray.

There were no mullas or qazis or hadjis;
No Sufis and no disciples of the Sufis,
No proud Kings, nor their subjects,
Nor Masters either, nor slaves.

There did not exist either the cult based on adoring **worship of** Vishnu,
Nor that based on Siva, the passive male,
And Sakti, the active female:
There was neither friendship nor sexual appetite;
God was both creditor and debtor then,
Such being His pleasure.

There had not been inscribed the Vedas,
Nor the Scriptures of the Semetics,
None read a gospel at dawn, an epistle at sunset,
Only the Unspeakable spoke of Himself to Himself.
Only the Unknowable of Himself had His knowledge.

When He so willed, He shaped the Universe;
The firmament He spread without a prop to support it.
He created the high gods, Brahma, Vishnu and Siva.
And Maya the goddess, the veil of illusion,
Who maketh Truth dark and increaseth worldly attachment.
To some, to a chosen few, the Guru revealeth the Lord's Word.
The Lord creates and He watcheth His Creation;
He made the heavenly bodies,
Our Universe in the endless space,
Above, below and around it.
And out of the Unmanifested, Unmovable ground of **His Being**,
To us and in us, He made Himself manifest.

None knoweth the Lord's beginning nor His end,
The True Guru revealeth but this secret:
Nānak, those whom the knowledge of the Lord
Maketh to wonder,
Are caught into His Truth,
Since singing His glory,
They become aware of His wonder.

Rag Maru, page 1035

44

haume kari tā tū nahī

Where Self exists,
God is not;
Where God exists,
There is no Self.
Sage, probe this mystery,
Of the immanence of the Lord in all that is,
Without the grace of the Guru
We could not know this essence of truth.

When we encounter the True Teacher,
And when the little Self dies,
Doubt and fear die with it,
And the pains of birth, death and rebirth,
The Guru's teaching is the highest wisdom
Since it shows us where our Liberator is.
Nānak repeats: 'I am that. That is I.'
The three worlds are included in that formula.

Rag Maru, Var, page 1092

45

BĀRĀMĀHĀ TUKHĀRĪ

(i)

CHET (*March-April*)

chet basant bhalā bhavar suhāvḍe

It is the month of Chet,
It is spring. All is seemly,

The beautiful honey-bee can be seen,
In the flower bedecked woodland,
The home of my childhood days.
But there is sorrow of separation in my soul,
Longingly I wait for the Lord;
If the husband comes not home, how can a wife
Find peace of mind?

The sorrow of separation wastes away my body,
The Koel calls in the mangoe groves,
Its notes are full of joy,
But there is a sorrow in my soul.
The honey-bee hovers about the blossoming bough,
A messenger of love and hope.
But O Mother of mine, it is like death to me,
For there is sorrow in my soul,
How shall I find peace and blessedness?

Spake the Guru:
Blessed peace would be attained in Chet,
If the Lord comes and meets the wife.

(ii)

VAISĀKH (*April–May*)

vaisakh bhalā sākhā ves kare

Beauteous Vaisākh,
When the bough adorns itself anew,
The wife awaits her Lord;
Her eyes fixed on the door,
'Come my Love, come have compassion for me,
Thou, my Love, alone can help me cross,
The turbulent waters of life; come home.
Without Thee I am as worthless as a shell,
Cast Thou Thine eyes upon me.
O who can make me worthy of Thee?
Who can make me win Thy love?
Who has seen my Love?
Who can show Him to me?'

Spake the Guru:
  Thou hast not far to go for the Lord,
  Know Him within thee, thou art His mansion.
  If thy body and soul yearn for the Lord,
  The Lord shall love thee;
  And Vaisākh appears beautiful;
  If thy mind is imbued with the Lord
  In Vaisākh you will meet the Lord you love.

(iii)

JETH (*May–June*)

māh jeth bhalā prītam kiu bisrai

Pleasant is the month of Jeth,
Why forget the Beloved Lord in such a month.
The lowland shimmers in the heat,
Like a forest on fire.
The wife prays:
Thy virtues I seek, Thy glory I sing
So that I may find favour in Thine eyes O Lord.
In the realm of Truth live Thou O Lord
Free from all attachment.

I can enter Thy mansion
If Thou permit me to be with Thee,
Without Thy grace
How can I, lowly, humble and helpless
Find the haven of rest and peace.

Spake the Guru
  In the month of Jeth
  She who knoweth the Lord
  Becometh like the Lord.
  She knoweth Him
  By treading the path of virtue.

(iv)

Asāḍ (June–July)

asāḍ bhalā sūraj gagan tape

In Asāḍ the sun scorches,
Skies are hot,
The earth burns like an oven,
Waters give up their vapours,
It burns and scorches the earth relentlessly.
In anguish the parched earth pines
Yet it fails not in its patient duty.

The sun's chariot passes the mountain tops;
Long shadows stretch across the land;
The housewife seeks the cool shades of the evening,
And the Cicadas give a shrill call from the glades;
If the comfort she seeks be in falsehood
There will be sorrow in store for her.
If it be in truth,
Here will be a life of joy.

Spake the Guru:
  My life and life's ending are at the will of the Lord
  To Him have I surrendered my soul.

(v)

SĀVAN (*July–August*)

sāvan sars manā ghan varsai

The season of rain has come;
My heart is full of joy,
My body and soul yearn for the Master,
But the Master is gone abroad.
If He return not, I shall die pining for Him.

The lightning strikes terror in my heart,
I stand all alone in my courtyard
In solitude and sorrow.

O Mother of mine, I stand on the brink of death.
Without the Lord I have no hunger nor no sleep,
I cannot suffer the clothes on my body.

Spake the Guru:
  She alone is the true wife,
  Who loses herself in the Lord.

(vi)

BHADON (*August–September*)

bhādoṅ bharm bhūli bhar joban pachtānī

Lost in the maze of falsehood,
I waste my wanton youth.
River and land are one expanse of water
For it is the monsoon, the season of merry-making.

It rains.
The nights are dark.
The wife knows no peace.
Peacocks cry with joy,
The papiha calls . . . peeoo, peeoo,
The fangs of serpents that crawl,
The stings of mosquitoes that fly
Are venomous.

The seas have burst their bounds in the ecstasy
Of fulfilment.
I alone am bereft of joy,
Without the love of the Beloved Lord.

Spake the Guru:
  Ask the Master who knows the way,
  Walk on the path which leads to the Lord.

(vii)

ASUN (*September–October*)

asun āu pirā sādhan jhūr mūi

O Master come to me,
I waste and will die.
If the Master wills,
I shall meet Him.
If He wills not,
I am drowned as in a deep well.
I strayed on to the paths of falsehood,
And the Master forsook me.
Age hath greyed my looks.
I have left many winters behind.
But the fires of hell still lie ahead.
Whither shall I turn?

The bough remaineth ever green.
For the sap that moveth within day and night,
Night and day, reneweth life.
If the Name of the Lord courseth in thy veins,
Life and hope will for ever be green.
That which cooketh slowly cooketh best.

Spake the Guru:
   It is trysting time O Lord,
   The True Guru now guides my steps to Thee.

(viii)

KATAK (*October–November*)

katak kirat paiyā jo prabh bhāe

What pleases the Lord,
Is all I merit.
The lamp of wisdom burneth steadily
If the soil that feeds it
Be reality.

If the oil that feeds the lamp
Be love,
The beloved will meet the Lord and be blessed.

If she dies full of faults
She will not find favour with the Lord.
Death after virtuous life will end her sorrow.

Those who are granted the worship of Thy Name
Merge in Thee, for Thou art then
Their aim and end in life.

Spake the Guru:
O Lord till Thou grant us vision
And burst the bonds of superstition
One watch of day will drag like half a year.

(ix)

MAGHAR (*November–December*)

maghar māh bhalā harigun aṅk samāva

The month of Maghar is bliss,
For her who is lost in the Lord.
She singeth the songs of joy and fulfilment
Why not love the Lord who is eternal?

He who is eternal, wise, omniscient is also the master of destiny.
The world is agitated because it hath lost faith in Him.
She that hath knowledge and contemplates
Loses herself in Him.
She loveth the Lord, the Lord loveth her.
In song and dance and verse
Let it be the Name of the Lord,
And sorrow will flee away.

Spake the Guru:
Only she is loved
Who worships the Lord not only outwardly
But worships with her soul.

(x)

POKH (*December–January*)

pokh tukhār pade van trin rās sokhai

As the winter's snow,
Freezes the sap in the tree and bush,
The absence of the Lord kills the body and the soul.
O Lord why comest not Thou?

He that gives life to all the world
Him I have realized through the Guru's Word.
His Light is in all the sources of life:
The egg, the womb, the sweat and the seed.
O Merciful God and Master; Give us Thy vision
That we may find salvation.

Spake the Guru:
    Only she mingles with Him
    Who loves the Lord, the giver of life.

(xi)

MAGH (*January–February*)

māgh punīt bhai tīrath antar jāniā

The Lord hath entered my being,
I make pilgrimage within myself and am purified,
I met Him.
He found me good
And let me lose myself in Him.

Beloved, if Thou findest me fair,
My pilgrimage is made,
My ablution done,
More than the sacred waters
Of Ganges, Yamuna and Tribeni mingled at the Sangam.
More than the seven seas.
All these and charity, alms giving and prayer
Is the knowledge of eternity that is the Lord.

Spake the Guru:
> He that hath worshipped the great giver of life
> Hath done more than bathe in the sixty and eight places of pilgrimage.

(xii)

PHALGUN (*February–March*)

phalgun man rehsī prem subhāe

> She whose heart is full of love,
> Is ever in full bloom.
> Day and night she lives in spiritual exaltation;
> She is in bliss because she hath no love of self.

> Only those that love Thee,
> Conquer love of Self.
> Come Thou graciously and abide in me.

> Many a lovely garment did I wear.
> The Master willed not and
> His palace doors were barred to me.
> When He wanted me I went
> With garlands and strings of jewels and raiment of finery.

Spake the Guru:
> A bride welcomed in the Master's mansion
> Hath found her true Lord and Love.

Rag Tukhari, pages 1107–10

46

sāligrām bip pūj manāvoh sukrit tulsī mālā

> Brahmin propitiate the saligram (Stone-God):
> By chaste conduct, not by telling thy beads.
> Repeat ever the Name of God.
> This is thy raft to cross life's unfathomable Ocean,
> Lord, have mercy upon us.

It is a waste of effort
To water a field of saltpetre;
A wall made of mud must collapse.
Why plaster it with cement?
The water wheel that will lift
From the well of thy soul
Is humility and service.
Water thy soul's garden,
Then the great Gardener
Shall find thee acceptable.

Root out the choking weeds
Of lust and anger;
Loosening the soil,
The more thou hoest and weedest,
The more lovely grows thy soul;
Love's labour is never lost;
The gawky crane is transformed
Into the graceful swan
Through the grace of God;
Nanak, lowest of the lowest, prays:
Lord, have mercy upon us.

Rag Basant, page 1171

47

kal hoī kute muhī khāj hoā murdār

In this age of darkness,
Men have become as dogs,
They eat the ill-gotten gains,
And bark out their lies;
Giving no thought to righteousness,
They have no honour in life,
And leave evil name after death.

Rag Sarang, page 1242

48

gyān vihūnā gāvai gīt

Some sing hymns without faith and knowledge,
As a mulla without means
Turns his own home into a mosque,
Or an idle-do-nothing can have his ears pierced,
Join a mendicant Order and lose his dignity;
That man who calls himself a teacher of truth,
But lives by begging, do not pay him homage;
The man who earns his bread by the sweat of his brow,
And gives some of his gains in charity
Knoweth, Nānak, the true way of life.

Var Sarang, page 1245

49

kulhān dinde bāvle lainde vade nilaj

Both the fool who confers authority on those that deserve not
And shameless those who accept it;
How can a mouse, dragging a winnowing basket
Tied to his waist behind him enter a hole?
The consecrators are mortal and the consecrated too;
Nānak without submitting to the Will of God,
No man knows whither he goes.
Mortals cannot consecrate or bless:

Our summer harvest is the one Eternal God,
Our winter harvest is the Lord's Holy Name,
These I reap as by right,
Since the Lord Himself has given me the title-deeds.
Many are the claims to authority that mortals make;
Many also are the beggars who live on scraps,
Many go into shades, having led such lives.

Rag Malar, page 1286

50
mast karon mūrakh jag kehīā

If I keep silent, men think me stupid,
If I talk much, how can I meditate on Thee?
Lord, who art the Judge of all I have left undone,
Without Thy Holy Name, there is no true piety.
Worldly men are so enmeshed in falsehood
That I love those who condemn me.

True piety is always condemned by the World,
Through the grace of God, the Word of the Guru,
Alone showeth us the path. He knoweth it
Who in his heart knoweth God as the Ground of all.

I am soiled; the Truth is spotlessly clean,
And alas, by repeating the Word: 'Excellent'
One does not attain to excellence oneself.
Thoughtlessly the self-centred man consumes poison;
But the man of God exalteth the Holy Name.

For the blind, the deaf, the slow-witted,
For the outcast, the thief and murderer, the wretched,
The love of the Lord's Name is glory and wealth:
The Holy Name for them is the only gold:
All of the world's wealth else venom and dust.

Some see goodness in others, some only fault:
Others concentrate entirely on the Word.
All these are God's gifts, and glory to Him.
All that is excellent, Lord, is Thy gift:
These words of Nānak are inspired by Thee.

Rag Prabhati, page 1330

51
jhad jhakhad ohāḍ

When under a sullen sky,
The strong wind lashed the sea into myriad waves,
Call, then, on the True Guru:
And fear not that thy ship will sink.

Slok Vadhik, page 1410, verse 4

52

so brahmin jo bindai brahm

A true Brahmin is one who grasps Brahm.
Meditation on God and self-control are his daily routine;
His religious observances are right conduct
And an unfretting heart.
He removes the sensual chains that bind the soul.
Such a Brahmin deserves all praise and honour.

Slok Vadhik, 16, page 1411

53

khatrī so jo karmā kā sūr

A true Kṣatriya, of the warrior caste, is one whose valour
Shows itself in every detail of his life.
The aim of his life is loving kindness,
Which he gives to the deserving,
And so becomes acceptable to God.
Any man who moved by greed, preaches falsehood,
In the end must pay the penalty for his deeds.

Slok Vadhik, 17, page 1411

54

pabar tū hariāvalā

O lotus flower, green was thy stalk, and golden thy beauty;
Through what fault of thine art thou now withered and brown?
Saith Nānak, A sickness hath blighted my body,
I am, like the lotus, deprived of the water
That has nourished me all my life.

Slok Vadhik, 30, page 1412

55

raj nā koī jīvīā

No mortal man lives long enough to exhaust his desires
Nor finds the path to his goal excessively long.
But the life everlasting
Is the life of the knowledge of truth.
Seek that within thyself.
For, little by little, in vanity,
Most men lay waste their lives;
Nānak, when death comes, unasked and unexpected,
Who shall bear the blame for such a waste?

Slok Vadhik, 31, page 1412

HYMNS OF GURU ANGAD DEV
(1504–1552)

ੴ

Guru Angad Dev, whose first name was Lehna, was the son of a trader. He was an ardent worshipper of Durga before he came under the influence of Guru Nānak. Nānak chose him as successor in preference to his own sons.

Guru Angad was the founder of Gurmukhi Script in which the Adi Granth is written. Sixty-two of his hymns are incorporated in the scripture. He died at the age of forty-eight, bequeathing the Guruship to his aged disciple Amar Das.

1

je sau candā ugvai sūraj cadai hazār

Were a thousand moons to arise,
Were a thousand suns to be shining.
All that external brightness
Would leave the world within, in darkness,
Unless it had the benign Guru's light.

Var Asa, page 463

2

nak nath khasam hath kirt dhake de

The nose-string of life is in the master's hands:
Our deeds drive us, and the truth is, Nānak,
That men must pasture where the Lord provides.

Var Sorath, page 653

3

milīa milyā nā milai

A union of bodies is no union,
However close it be,
It is only when souls meet
Can we speak of a union true.

Var Suhi, page 791

4

nānak tinā basant hai jin ghar vasiā kant

For those, O Nānak, it is perpetual spring,
With whom the Beloved dwelleth as in their homes;
But day and night burn with desire
Those whose Beloved is in distant lands.

Var Suhi, page 791

5

so kion andhā ākhīa:

Why call them blind,
Whom nature has robbed of sight;
He that hath not discovered the divine will,
Nānak, he is truly blind.

Var Ramkali, page 954

6

āp upāe nānakā āpe rakhe vek

He Himself is the Creator;
He Himself for all His creatures,
Sets different places.
Whom should I despise,
Since the one Lord made us all?
There is one Master of all things,
He setteth each man to his task
And watcheth over all men.
Some have great tasks, some little tasks,
No one departeth unrewarded.
Naked man comes into the earth,
Naked he departeth hence;
In between he toils to make a show.
O Nānak, the man who understandeth not the Will of God,
How shall he bear himself on death's call.

Var Sarang, page 1237

7

kathā kahānī bedī ānī pāp pun vicār

The Vedic scholars have handed down to us,
A traditional mythology and have also defined
The doctrines of sin, virtue and retribution.
For what men give they receive.
And for what they receive a gift shall be required of them.

And reaping as they have sowed
They are accordingly reborn,
Either in hell or heaven.
According to actions of past lives,
Men they say, are born in high castes and low,
Yet the world wandereth in doubt as to all this.

But the ambrosial Word of the Guru,
Speaketh of that which is real,
And bringeth knowledge of the Divine,
And bringeth the inner pondering of it.
The saints speak of it,
The saints know it.
They who possess divine knowledge
Ponder inwardly over its Light.

God by His Will made the world,
God at His Will controlleth it;
He beholdeth all things set under His Will.
Nānak, if before a man dies.
He can cast down his ego,
He shall not in the sight of the Lord go unregarded.

Var Sarang, page 1243

8

nāu fakīrai pātsāh mūrakh pandit nāu

Every beggar today would be a King,
Every blockhead sets up as a Pundit;
The blind man would be a connoisseur of gems,
That is the modern way of talking of things;
The really bad man sets up as a spiritual leader;
The liar is judged the perfect type of man;
So it is in this iron age; But, Nānak, even now
The Guru can teach us how to choose among men.

Var Malar, page 1288

nānak dunyā kīa vadiāyāṅ agī setī jāl

Nānak, burn in the fire
All the glories of the world;
These accursed things
Have made men forget
The Holy Name of the Lord;
Not one of them will accompany thee,
Beyond the gate of darkness.

Var Malar, page 1290

3

HYMNS OF GURU AMAR DAS
(1479-1574)

Amar Das's conversion to Sikh faith is said to have occurred after his hearing a recitation of Nānak's Japji. He remained with Guru Angad for the last six years of the latter's life and succeeded him in 1552 when he was himself an old man of seventy-three.

Amar Das organized the scattered Sikh congregations into twenty-two dioceses and appointed spiritual mentors for each, some of whom were women. He was a great reformer. He made communal dining compulsory amongst Sikhs converted from different castes of Hindus and Muslims and forbade the practice of Satī amongst his followers.

Amar Das contributed 907 verses to the Adi Granth, all of which were written between the age of seventy-three when he became a Guru, and ninety-five when he died.

I

THE ANAND SAHIB

(i)

anand bheā merī māe

Rejoice with me, O mother,
That I have found the True Guru,
The True Guru have I found without penance,
And songs of rejoicings are in my heart.
The excellent Rāgās and the race of the heavenly Muses
Have come to sing hymns to the Lord;
Those in whose hearts the Lord indwelleth,
Sing the Song of praise to Him.
Saith Nānak: My heart is full of joy
That I have found the True Guru.

(ii)

eh man meriā tū sadā rauh hari nāle

O my mind, abide thou ever with God,
Abide with God, O my soul,
Who will make thee to forget all thy sorrow,
Thou shalt be acceptable unto the Lord.
He will manage all thine affairs for thee;
The Lord is Perfect and in all things all-powerful;
Why shouldst thou ever forget the Lord?
Saith Nānak: O my mind,
Abide thou ever with God.

(iii)

sace sahiba kia nahi ghar tere

O my True Lord, What is there
That is not to be found in Thy House?
In Thy House are all riches;
He to whom Thou givest receiveth,
He will sing Thy Glories for ever,
And house Thy Name in his heart.

Heavenly Music resoundeth,
In the hearts where the Lord indwelleth;
Saith Nanak: O my true Lord,
What is there, that is not to be found in Thy House.

(iv)

sācā nām merā adhāro

Thy Name, O Lord, is my sustenance,
Only on the True Name, which quieteth all my hungers do I live;
The true Name, abiding in my heart,
Hath granted me peace and joy,
And fulfilled all my desires.
I am ever a sacrifice unto the Guru,
Whose gifts these are.
Saith Nānak: Listen, O Saints, love the Word.
Thy Name, O Lord, is my sustenance.

(v)

vaje panc sabad tit ghar subhāge

Celestial Music is heard in the blessed house,
The heart, where God indwelleth;
In that happy house,
In which God hath put forth His strength;
Heavenly Music is heard.
Therein the Lord has subdued the five evil passions,
And destroyed the fear of death.
Saith Nānak: They obtain happiness
And in their hearts the heavenly Music is heard.

(vi)

sācī livai bin deh nimāṅī

Without true love there is no honour for this mortal body
This mortal body is without honour if without love;
Besides Thee, Lord, there is none other all-powerful;

What can the wretched creature do? Have mercy on us, Lord.
For mortal man there is no other refuge but Thy Name.
By love of the Name the soul can be made beautiful;
Saith Nānak: What can the wretched creature do,
Without the love of the Lord.

(vii)

anand anand sabh ko kahe

All men talk of bliss, but true bliss,
Can only be got by keeping the company of the Guru;
It is through the grace of the Guru,
That eternal bliss can be known.
In his mercy the Guru destroyeth all sins,
And he putteth on the eyes the salve of divine knowledge,
Those who in their inner hearts have achieved detachment from the world
The True One hath made holy with the Word.
Saith Nānak: That is the true bliss,
That can be got by keeping the company of the Guru.

(viii)

bhagtān kī cāl nirālī

The path of the saint is a strange path;
The path of the saint is strange indeed,
He walketh by a hard road;
He renounces avarice, greed, self-will,
And attachment to the goods of the world;
And he maketh but little use of speech;
He walketh by a way sharper than a sword's edge,
By a way narrower than a hair's breadth.
By the grace of the Guru,
The desires of those who renounce self-will
Are set upon the Lord.
Saith Nānak: In every age, the path of the Saint
Is a strange path.

(ix)

karamī sahaj na ūpjai

Knowledge of the Transcendent is not to be obtained,
Through outward religious observances, without knowledge,
Doubt and delusion will not depart;
No amount of outward observances
Will remove doubt and delusion.
The mind is filthy with ignorance,
How can it be made clean?
Wash thy mind, O man, in the light of the Word,
And fix thy heart and thy soul upon the Lord.
Saith Nānak: It is by the grace of the Guru
That knowledge of the Transcendent is obtained.
In this way only will doubt and delusion depart.

(x)

jion maile bhāron nirmal

Those who, impure within, seem pure outwardly,
Fair without and foul within, have gambled their lives away,
They have contracted the vile disease of desire;
They have forgotten they are mortal.
Though the Name of the Lord
Is the most precious thing in the scriptures,
To that they attend not,
And they wander wildly like demons.
Saith Nānak: That man who hath discarded truth
And attached himself to falsehood hath gambled his life away.

(xi)

jion nirmal bāhron nirmal

Those who, pure within, are also pure without,
Who are fair without and fair within, act virtuously,
Through the grace of the True Guru,
They have not heard even the name of falsehood;
All their hopes are set upon the Truth;

Blessed are such traders in virtue,
Who have earned the jewel of life.
Saith Nānak: Those who are pure within
Abide ever with the True Guru.

(xii)

eh sarīrā meriā is jag mai āe ke

O my body, what hast thou brought to pass,
In thy sojourn on this earth? What hast thou done,
   O body,
Since thy coming into the world?
To the Lord who shaped thee,
Thou hast given no place in thine heart.
It is through the Guru's grace
That the Name in the heart indwelleth.
The Lord's Name in the heart
Is the gift of past good deeds.
Saith Nānak: That mortal human body is acceptable
That hath set its heart upon the True Guru.

(xiii)

eh netro merio har tum mai jot dharī

O mine eyes, it was the Lord who gave ye Light,
Look on none but Him,
Look on none but the Lord;
By His grace will you see Him,
The world which appeareth so poisonous to you,
Is the manifestation of God.
When by the grace of the Guru I was granted
   understanding
I saw that there is One God.
And I saw that there is no other beside Him.
Saith Nānak: These eyes of mine were blind,
But when I met the True Guru,
They were graced with divine Light.

(xiv)

anand suno vadhbhāgio

Listen, O fortunate ones, to my joyful Song,
And all the desires of your hearts shall be fulfilled;
When we grasp the Lord in His uttermost supremacy,
All griefs must then go from us;
Through listening to the True Word
My griefs, my sicknesses, my torments have departed;
The saints and the holy are filled with joy
When they hear the word from the True Teacher;
He who heareth the Word is made pure;
He who speaketh the Word is made holy,
The True Guru filleth all their beings.
Nānak proclaimeth: For those who prostrate themselves
At the True Teacher's feet, the heavenly Music soundeth.

Rag Ramkali, pages 917–22: 3, 5, 7, 10, 14, 18, 19, 20, 35, 36, 40.

2

man tu jot sarup hai

Mind, thou art a Spark of Divine Light, so grasp the True Source of thy being.
The Lord is ever with thee; through the Guru's teachings rejoice in His Presence.
By grasping thine own true nature, thou graspest God's,
And the meaning of birth and death.
When through the Guru's grace thou hast grasped the Supreme One
Thou shalt lose the illusion of otherness.
Thou shalt abide in peace, honoured, and acceptable.
Nānak saith: O my mind, thou art an image of God,
Grasp the True Source of thy being.

Rag Asa, 441

3

rām rām sabh ko kahai

All men cry 'Lord, Lord'.
But by vain repetition man is not made one with the Lord.
It is only when, by the grace of the Guru, God in the heart indwelleth,
That human effort bears fruit.
He who loveth the Lord from his heart's core
Shall never forget him, but from his heart and soul
Shall ever repeat the Lord's Name.
They who are deceivers in their hearts but outwardly ape holiness
Shall not lose their lusts, and shall grieve at the time of departure.
However strenuously a man may wash himself
At the many holy places,
It is not thus that self-will is cleansed from him!
The King of Death, Dharmraj, shall chastise him
Who hath not cast down his self-will.
Only by the Guru's grace shall man meet God and understand Him!
Nānak saith: The man who destroyeth his own self-will
Shall certainly meet God!

Rag Gujri, 491

4

nānak giānī jag jītā

Nānak, the man of divine knowledge hath conquered the world,
Which itself hath conquered all other men:
Through the Name, his affairs prosper.
And all his actions are as the Lord willeth.
Through the Guru's teaching his mind is steadfast and none can shake it.
God Himself standeth by him, and all that he doth is beautiful.
The perverse have been led astray from the Lord
By greed, by avarice, by proud self-will.
Day and night, they wrangle; they contemplate not the True Word.

The Lord hath taken away from them their good understanding;
So all their conversation is sinful.
In their hearts are avarice and the pitch black of ignorance;
However much they are given, their desires are insatiable.
Nānak saith: It is wise to break with the perverse
Who are attached to the illusory goods of the world.

Rag Bihagra, Var, 548

5

mun maile sabh kich mailā

If the mind is unclean, all else is unclean;
And ceremonial washings cannot wash the mind.
This world is the realm of illusion:
There are few who grasp the Real.
O my mind, remember the Holy Name!
That is the precious gift of the Guru to men.
Were a man to learn all the postures of the most austere Yogis,
And mortify all his senses,
Not so would he cleanse the mind, or discard self-will.
There is no cure for the mind's sickness
But taking shelter at the Guru's feet.
To meet the Guru is to experience
A change of outlook that cannot be described.
Saith Nānak: From the mind of him who dies to self
Through meeting the Guru, and is reborn through the Guru's Word,
All uncleanness is removed.

Vadhans, page 558

6

haumain nāvain nāl virodh hai

Self-will is opposed to the Holy Name. The two cannot dwell in one house.
None can serve in a state of self-will, and the self-willed mind is worthless.
O my mind, fix thyself upon God's Name, and practise the Guru's Word.

By obeying God's Will, thou graspest Him, and sheddest thy self-will.
Self-will is the cause of all shapes and their coming into being:
It is the source of illusion, and veils the Reality from us.
The self-willed man cannot love God or understand His Will;
The soul is imprisoned in self-will and the Name cannot dwell in the heart.
But when a man meets the True Guru his self-will is destroyed,
And then the Truth alighteth in his heart to abide there
So, practising truth, a man lives in Truth
And, serving God who is Truth, is absorbed in Him.

Rag Vadhans, page 560

7

satgur no sabh ko vekhdā

All men have access to the Guru
But a mere glimpse of the Guru does not save them;
Without understanding of the Guru's Word
The self is not made clean nor the love of the Name implanted;
Some through God's Grace give up all self-will and sinfulness
And are made one with God:
Others, saith Nānak, at the sight of the Guru
Die to self, through the Guru's love,
And are at once made one with the Divine Spirit.

Rag Vadhans, page 594

8

janam janam kī is man ko mal lāgī

Soiled by its former births the soul is as black as jet:
Like an oily rag that could not be clean, were it washed a hundred times!
But if through the Guru's Grace a man dies to self
And be born to new understanding,
Then the soul is free from its soiling, and is not born again.

Rag Sorath, Var, page 651

9

satiaṅ eh nā ākhian

It is not they who burn themselves alive
With their husband's dead bodies, who are *Satīs*,
Nānak, they rather are Satīs,
Whom the shock of separation from their husbands kill;
They also are known as Satīs,
Who abide in modesty and contentment;
Who wait upon the Lord
And ever rising in the morning remember Him.

Rag Suhi, Var, page 787

10

dhan pir eh na akhian

They are not truly husband and wife,
Whose bodies merely come together;
Only they are truly wedded
When two bodies have one soul.

Var Suhi, page 788

11

jagat jalandā rakh lai apnī kirpā dhūr

Save this world consumed in fire,
O Lord, with Thy gracious Mercy!
Save it in any way it can be saved!
The Satguru hath shown the path of peace
In the contemplation of the True Word.
Nānak knoweth none besides God
Who is the only Saviour.

Var Bilawal, page 853

12

mūrakh hovai so sunai mūrakh kā kehnā

Only a fool listens to an ignorant fool.
But what, may one ask, is the sign of a fool?
And how does he conduct himself?
A fool is a stupid creature
Whose soul is sick with self-love.
Leading such a life he suffers,
And his life is continual suffering.
If the poor thing is about to fall in a well
Who, really, can save him?

But the man who seeks truth takes life seriously,
He lives in detachment, Nānak,
He does what pleases God, the saint
Accepts whatever happens to him
As being God's Will.
Var Ramkali, page 953

13

jāt kā garb nā kerīo koī

Let no man be proud because of his caste.
For the man who graspeth God in his heart
He, no other, is the true Brahmin:
So, O fool, about thy caste be not vainglorious!
From vainglory emerge too many of the mind's evils!
Though they say there are four castes
One God created all men:
All men were moulded out of the same clay,
The Great Potter hath merely varied the shapes of them.
All men are mixed of the same five elements,
No one can make any element less in one, more in another.
Man is born in chains:
Without meeting the True Guru,
He cannot attain liberation.
Rag Bhairon, page 1128

14

basant cadiā phūlī banrāe

With the coming of spring,
There is blossom on every spray;
In the same fashion,
With the coming of inner devotion to God,
All sentient creatures have an inner blossoming,
And in this way the mind becometh fresh and green.
Day and night repeating the Name of the Lord,
Those who have seen God wash away all self-will!
The True Guru hath given to mankind
The Holy word and the hymns:
The whole world blossometh with love through the True Guru.
Life beareth flowers and fruits when the Lord willeth it:
It is by the devotion to the Lord, the source of life,
That the True Guru is attained.
The Lord Himself is the springtime
And the world is His Garden.
Only through His gracious gift to us
Can we attain the blessing of devotion to Him solely.

Rag Basant, page 1177

15

babīhā nā billāe nā tarsāe

O babīhā, wail not and cry not for water:
Let thy mind abide by His Will!
Only by abiding by His Will, saith Nānak,
Will all thirsts be slaked
And love and joy fourfold attained.

Rag Malar, Var, page 1282

16

satgur purkh nirvair hai

The True Guru, the divine one, is without enmity.
He fixeth his heart ever on God.

If a man should hate the Guru who is without hatred,
Such a man setteth fire to his own house;
Wrath and self-will are within him,
Day by day he burneth in their flames,
Living ever in agony and grief.
The wicked bark like dogs, telling lies;
Pursuing worldly gains, they swallow poison;
Shamelessly they go begging from door to door,
Asking for what will make them ill;
They are like the sons of a whore
Who cannot name their father.
They remember not the Name of God.
God Himself has confounded them;
When He takes mercy upon those gone astray,
He will unite them to Himself through the Guru.
The humble Nānak is a sacrifice to any man
Who taketh refuge at the feet of the Guru.

Slok Vadhik, 23, page 1415

17

asī khate bahut kamānvde

Our transgressions are past counting,
There is no end to our sins,
Be merciful, Forgive us, O Lord:
We are great sinners and wrongdoers.
There is no hope of our redemption.
O Lord, dear Lord, our deeds weighed in the balance
Would get us no place in Thy Court!
Forgive us and make us one with Thyself
Through the grace of the Guru.
If the Lord God can be attained to,
Then all evil is destroyed.
Victory, O Nānak, be unto them
Who meditate on His Name!

Slok Vadhik, 29, page 1416

18

sabd marai soī jan sijhai

He who dies in the Word
Attains to success.
Without the Word
None can be saved.
Man lives like a hypocrite,
The victim of his own acts:
Man is destroyed
By worldly attachments.
O Nānak, without the Guru
The Name cannot be known,
The Word's spirit cannot be known
However a man may crave for it.

Slok Vadhik, 32, page 1416

19

lobhī kā visāh nā kījai

Trust not the avaricious man.
He will deceive you, drive you into a corner
Where you are helpless.
A man only shames himself
By keeping company with the self-willed;
The avaricious are shamed,
They will depart from here
Having wasted their lives.
They have wrecked their lives.

Lord, give us the company
Of Thy holy saints
So that our hearts may become
Receptive of Thy Name.
The dross of life and death
Can be washed away, saith Nānak,
By singing the Lord's Praises!

Slok Vadhik, 40, page 1417

20

gurmukh budhe kade·nā hovaī

The souls whom the Guru has enlightened
Do not fall into decay.
They are absorbed in the praises of God.
And their understanding hath been shaped
By the Divine Knowledge.
With their minds fixed on the Transcendent one
For they live ever in blissful comprehension
For them joy and sorrow are one,
Since they see the One everywhere
Whose spirit pervades all things.

Slok Vadhik, 44, page 1418

4

HYMNS OF GURU RAM DAS
(1534–1581)

ੴ

Ram Das was the son-in-law of Guru Amar Das. He founded the city of Amritsar and dug the tank which later became the site of the Golden Temple.

He has contributed 679 hymns to the *Adi Granth*.

1

har andar bāhar ik tū

Thou art the only one within us and without us,
Thou knowest each heart's secrets; mortal man,
God is aware of every deed thou doest.
Recollect Him, ever, and hold Him in contemplation;
The sinner lives in fear, the good are happy.
Thou, Lord, art Truth and on Truth is built Thy Justice,
Why should the good man fear? O Nānak, those
Who have grasped the Truth will at last become one with Truth.

Var Sri Rag, page 84

2

mātā prīt kare put khāe

A mother loves to watch her son eat,
A fish loves to be always in water,
The true Guru loves to see his Sikhs.
O Lord make us of the holy company
On meeting whom all our sorrows are vanquished:
As a cow shows love to her strayed calf on finding it;
As a wife shows love to her husband when he comes home,
So those who love the Lord are delighted
When they sing the praises of the Lord.
The Chatrik loves the rain drops;
The King loves his wealth and imperial power;
The worshipper of the Lord
Loves only to meditate on the Lord Infinite.
The worldly man desires to amass wealth:
The Guru's disciple longs for his Master's embrace:
Nānak, the slave, desires to kiss
The feet of the saints of God.

Rag Gauri, page 164

3

hamre man cit har ās nit kio dekhā har dars tūmārā

Deep in me there is a longing to see Thee, O my Beloved!
The Lord who hath given me the grace of love for Him
Knoweth how deep is my love. I would be a sacrifice to the
  Guru
Who has made me at one with the Lover Who dwelt afar!
Lord, I am a sinner seeking sanctuary at Thy Gates
In the hope that even I, utterly without merit,
May through Thy Grace be blessed with union with Thee.
Our sins are unnumbered: no count to our errors:
Thou, who art Justice, art also Mercy, O Lord.
Cleanse me, O Lord, of my stains, as it may please Thee.
I am a sinner saved by the Guru's society:
He has saved me by bearing witness to the Holy Name!
O True Guru, how can I speak of thy virtues?
When thou but speakest, I am transported with wonder.
Who, but the True Guru, could save a sinner like me?
Guru, thou art my father and my mother,
Thou art my friend, and hast wrought my salvation,
Thou art my most precious peace, and best knowest my soul!
Here below I was a wanderer and helpless,
None cared for me, but even I, wretch, have found honour
Through the society of the True Guru.
Glory, glory to the True Guru, saith Nānak,
Since, in his company,
Sorrow and pain have departed!

Rag Gauri, page 167

4

gur satgur kā jo sikh akhāe

He who deems himself a Sikh of the true Guru
Should rise betimes and contemplate the Name.
In the early hours of the morning he should rise and bathe
And cleanse his soul in a tank of nectar,
As he repeats the Name the Guru taught him.
Thus he washes away the sins of his soul.

Then at dawn he should sing the hymns of the Guru.
And throughout all the busyness of the day
He should hold in his heart the Name.
He who repeats the Name with every breath
Such a Sikh is indeed dear to the Guru:
The Sikh that wins the favour of the Lord
Has received the gift of the Lord's Name from the Guru.
Nānak seeks to kiss the dust under the feet of such a Sikh
Who utters the Name and inspires others to do so!

Gauri, Var, page 305

5

jin ke cit kathor hain

The hard of heart
Delight not in the company of the True Guru.
Truth prevails in his presence, the charlatans
Are restless, and go out and seek bad company.
Where Truth prevails, there is no place for falsehood.
The lovers of evil should seek the company of Evil:
The lovers of Truth should seek for the True Guru.

Var Gauri, page 314

6

manmukh mūloṅ bhuliā

The self-centred man from the start took the wrong path:
He gave himself up to greed, to attachment and to pride:
He wasted his days in wrangling, and thought not on the Word.
The Lord seems to have deprived him of all.
His speech is sinful. The world's wealth cannot satisfy him,
Desire still burns fiercely within him
And his ignorance is as the darkness of a cave.
Nānak saith: Comradeship with such self-centred people
Who care for nothing but the pleasures of this world
Is best brought to an end!

Var Gauri, page 316

7

kis hī dhaḍā kīa mitār sut nāl bhāī

Some make a pact with
Brothers, sons, and friends;
Others work in with
Their son-in-law and his parents.
Others join in factions,
With their landlords and the nobles
For selfish ends.
I have made a pact with God, I rely on Him only
Who pervades all things.

I am of God's faction:
He is my mainstay.
I am of no other group besides God's:
I sing only of His Infinite Virtues.
All these human powers men make their pacts with
Are subject to death and decay.
They are dishonest and without scruple,
They will not stick to anyone, so a man
Should always repent of joining such false factions.
I have made a pact with the Supreme Lord,
Unequalled in His Power.

All other pacts are for worldly power:
For worldly gains the fools dispute and struggle.
Subject to birth and death, they stake life.
I am of the Lord's faction,
Who can look after me in this world and the next.

In the Kali age, five dominant passions cause factions:
Lust, anger, greed, attachment, self-will.
But he whom the Lord blesseth with His Grace
Meets Him through keeping the company of Truth.
I am in the Lord's faction,
Who has destroyed all other factions.

False is all love besides that of God
That divides men into warring groups.
The many factions decry and malign each other
And vanity consumes them.
As a man sows, so must he reap.
Nānak hath signed a bond with Righteousness
That can conquer the whole world.

Rag Asa, page 366

8

har amrit bhine loiṇā

My eyes are wet with the Lord's nectar; my soul is drenched in His Love.
He tested my heart with His touchstone: He found it pure
Through the Guru my soul and body are dyed as with deep crimson.
Nānak, the slave, has made himself fragrant with musk:
My earthly life is blessed.

The hymn of the Lord's love is like a pointed arrow,
That hath pierced deep in my heart: who feels love's pain knows it
And he that dies to this life even while living
Has obtained his deliverance even in this life.
Saith Nānak: By meeting the True Guru
Life's dangerous ocean is crossed.

Ignorant and a fool though I am, I seek thy sanctuary
May I attain to the love of my Beloved!
I reached God through the perfect Guru: may I seek nothing but His service.
My mind and body are soothed, O Lord, by Thy Word:
I repeat Thy Holy Name with thrilling delight.
Through meeting the saints and seeking Truth in their company
Nānak has attained to God.

Hear my prayer, O Thou who hast pity on the wretched!
I seek my shelter in the Name; I long for the Name to be on my lips.

O Lord, it is Thy Greatness to love Thy Saints and save the honour.
Humble Nānak has taken Thee as his stronghold:
Thy Name has helped him to cross the dangerous ocean.

Rag Asa, page 448

9

mero sunder kaho milai kit galī

Tell me in what street I shall find my Beauteous Lord?
O Saints of God, show me the way I should follow.
The words of the Beloved fill my heart with sweetness,
And I long to follow this pain. Though I am short
And my hair is dishevelled, if the Lord desireth me
Even I become beautiful and I melt in His Embrace.
There is but one Beloved; all souls are as brides that seek His Love;
She who winneth the Lord's love is beautiful.
What can the slave Nānak do,
But walk in the way
That pleaseth the Lord?

Dev Gandhari, page 527

10

ab hum calī ṭhakar pai hār

Now, the Lord is my last refuge.
Lord! I have sought safety at thy feet:
Save me or slay me, as it please Thee, Lord!
The world's deceitful honours I have cast in the fire,
What do I care if man blame or praise me?
Unto the Lord I have devoted my whole being.
He, Lord, who seeks refuge in Thee
Through Thine Infinite Mercy Thou art his salvation.
Nānak, Thy slave, seeketh refuge in Thee:
Hide my shame, O Lord!

Dev Gandhari, page 527

11

ham bārak kachue nā jāne

Lord, I am Thy child, and know nothing of Thy Greatness.
I am ignorant and a fool. Lord, have mercy,
Bless me with Thy High Wisdom: change a silly child to a sage.
My indolent mind had nodded and fallen to slumber.
By the grace of God I met the Guru!
By whom my spirit was illumined.
O Guru, inspire me with everlasting love of God
And make the Name of the Lord my life-breath.
O Guru, without the Name of the Lord I would die:
It is to me what wine is to the drunkard.

Those to whom it has been granted to love God
Heap the reward of good deeds in past lives;
I bow and I kiss the feet of those
Who made me love the Lord.
My Lord was merciful, after long parting my soul again encountered Him.
Hail, hail, to the True Guru; who has established me with his Word.
Nānak is a sacrifice unto Him.

Jaitsiri, page 697

12

koi ān milavai merā prītam piārā

I will be as the slave of him
Who bringeth the Beloved for my tryst,
I longed to glimpse the Beloved. By God's Grace
I met the Guru and I attained to
Contemplation of the Name.

Lord, when I am happy, I shall worship Thee, only:
When I suffer, I shall not forget Thee.
Though Thou shouldst cause me to hunger
I should live like a man full-fed:
Through my suffering I should feel joy.

For Thee, I would tear this sentient frame to pieces
And let it be devoured by flames.
For Thee, I would live as the humblest of servants:
Fetching Thy Saints water, and fanning them in the heat,
Eating what scraps Thou wouldst grant me.
Thy slave Nānak is prone at Thy Outer Gates:
Vouchsafe to me only a glimpse of Thee in Thy Glory!

I would tear out my eyes and place them beneath Thy feet,
I would walk barefoot round the world could I but encounter
  Thee.
Beloved, shouldst Thou seat me near Thee
Only for Thyself would I have adoration.
Shouldst Thou expel me with violence from Thy Presence,
Still Thee, and Thee alone, should I contemplate.

Lord, if the people praise me, it is Thy Praise,
Should they slander and curse me, Beloved, I would not leave
  Thee!
When I am protected by Thee, who can do aught against me?
But should I ever forget Thee, then let me die!
For the Guru I would let myself be sacrificed, again and again;
I would lie prone at his feet to win his love.
Lord, Thy slave Nānak is mad with love of Thee:
Mad to catch a glimpse of Thee, O Lord!

Be there gale and storm and torrential rain,
Even then I would set forth to meet the Guru!
Be there the breadth and the depth of waters between them,
A Sikh would cross the ocean to meet his Guru.
As a man dies of thirst when deprived of water,
So a Sikh also dies when deprived of his Guru.
As the parched earth is fresh after a shower
So a Sikh is full of delight on meeting his Guru.
O Lord, I would be a servant of Thy Servants:
I would call on Thee from afar with a humble cry.
Nānak prayeth to the Lord he loveth:
May I attain the height of joy on encountering the Guru.

Lord, Thou art the Guru, Thou art his disciple:
Venerating the Guru, truly I worship Thee!

Those that worship Thee, Lord, become what Thou art:
Thou hast ever bestowed honour on the love of Thy Saints.
Thy Treasury is a Treasure-House of Devotions:
Thou givest the gift of loving Thee to him whom Thou favourest.
None can love Thee except through the gift of Thy Grace:
Mere human wisdom to reach Thee is of no avail.
By contemplating the Guru everlastingly
The slumbering spirit is awakened.
Wretched Nānak, Lord, asks but one gift of Thee:
Let me humbly serve the Saints who serve Thee!

Should the Guru rebuke me, sweet would be his rebuking:
Should he then forgive me, that would be His glory, indeed!
What the man instructed by the Guru says has meaning:
What the self-willed man says is meaningless and vain.
In the coldest winter, frost-bound, the snow falling,
A Sikh will still set out to meet his Guru.
Day and night, might I delight in the vision of the Guru:
I would like to place his lotus feet on my eyelids!
All that a man can do I would for the Guru:
What pleaseth the Guru is accepted by God.
Day and night might I contemplate the feet of the Guru:
Send like a shower Thy Mercies on me, O Lord!
To Nānak, the Guru is as his soul and his substance:
On meeting the Guru, all his desires are fulfilled.
The Lord, Nānak's Lord, pervadeth the whole universe:
Here and there and everywhere he seeth the Lord.

Rag Suhi, page 757

13

THE MARRIAGE HYMNS (LĀVĀN)

har pehladī lānv parvirt

By the first nuptial circling
The Lord sheweth ye His Ordinance for the daily duties of wedded life:
The Scriptures are the Word of the Lord,
Learn righteousness through them,
And the Lord will free ye from sin.

Hold fast to righteousness,
Contemplate the Name of the Lord,
Fixing it in your memory as the scriptures have prescribed.
Devote yourselves to the Perfect and True Guru,
And all your sins shall depart.
Fortunate are those whose minds
Are imbued with the Sweetness of His Name,
To them happiness comes without effort;
The slave Nānak proclaimeth
That in the first circling
The marriage rite hath begun.

(ii)

By the second nuptial circling
Ye are to understand that the Lord
Hath caused ye to meet the True Guru,
The fear in your hearts has departed;
The filth of selfness in your minds is washed away,
By having the fear of God and by singing His Praises.
I stand before Him with reverence,
The Lord God is the soul of the universe:
There is naught that He doth not pervade.
Within us and without, there is One God only:
In the company of Saints
Then are heard the songs of rejoicing.
The slave Nānak proclaimeth
That in the second circling
Divine Music is heard.

(iii)

In the third circling
There is a longing for the Lord
And detachment from the world.
In the company of the Saints,
By our great good fortune,
We encounter the Lord.
The Lord is found in His purity
Through His exaltation,
Through the singing of His hymns.
By great good fortune we have lighted,

On the company of the Saints
Wherein is told the story
Of the Ineffable Lord.
The Holy Name echoes in the heart,
Echoes and absorbs us:
We repeat the Name of the Lord,
Being blessed by a fortunate destiny
Written from of old on our foreheads.
The slave Nānak proclaimeth
That in the third circling
The love of God has been awakened in the heart.

(iv)

In the fourth circling
The mind reaches to knowledge of the Divine
And God is innerly grasped:
Through the Grace of the Guru
We have attained with ease to the Lord;
The sweetness of the Beloved
Pervades us, body and soul.
Dear and pleasing is the Lord to us:
Night and day our minds are fixed on Him.
By exalting the Lord
We have attained the Lord:
The fruit our hearts desired;
The Beloved has finished His work.
The soul, the spouse, delighteth in the Beloved's Name.
Felicitations fill our minds;
The Name rings in our hearts:
The Lord God is united with His Holy Bride.
The heart of the Bride flowers with His Name.
The slave Nānak proclaimeth
That in the fourth circling
We have found the Eternal Lord.

Rag Suhi, page 773

14

har darṣan ko merā man bauh tapte

As a thirsting man yearneth for water
So longeth deeply my soul for the sight of the Lord,
Love of the Lord, like an arrow, hath pierced my heart.
Only my Beloved knoweth my pain and how I suffer within.
Any man who can tell me of my Beloved
Shall be my comrade and my brother.
Gather ye, comrades, and join with me in praising the Lord!
Since I have followed the wise counsel of the Guru,
Lord, grant Thy servant, Nānak, this one desire:
Let me behold Thee, and body and soul have peace!

Rag Gond, page 861

15

vāh vāh satgur purkh hai

Hail, all hail, to the True Guru, the Perfect,
Who hath grasped the Highest Truth!
On encountering the Guru, every thirst is slaked.
Body and mind are freshened.
Hail, all hail, to the Guru, to Truth Incarnate,
In whose just eyes all are alike.
Hail, all hail, to the True Guru, free from enmity,
Above the need of praise or the fear of calumny.
Hail, all hail, to the True Guru, the Wise,
Who hath God's Light within him.
Hail, all hail, to the True Guru, the Eternal,
Whose goal is beyond our grasping.
Hail, all hail, to the True Guru, the True,
Who confirmeth men in the Truth.
Hail, all hail, to the True Guru, saith Nānak.
It is he who imparteth the Word.

Slok Vadhik, page 1421

HYMNS OF GURU ARJAN DEV
(1563-1606)

Arjan Dev was the youngest son of Guru Ram Das. He built the Golden Temple at Amritsar and compiled the *Adi Guru Granth*. Suspecting that he had helped his rebellious son Khusrau, Jahangir had him arrested and ordered him to be put to death. He was the first martyr of Sikh history.

There are 2218 verses by Guru Arjan in the *Adi Granth*.

I. THE 'SUKHMANĪ'

The Hymn of Peace

1

ād gure nameh jugād gure name

Hail to the Founder Guru, to the Primal One,[1]
Hail to the Guru Eternal,
Hail to the Satguru: Truth's Embodiment
Hail to the Gurudev: holy and divine.

Aṣṭapadī, 1; *Slok*, 1

2

simroṅ simar simar sukh pāvoṅ

Ever and ever, remembering, remember Thy Lord:
In whose remembrance thou shalt attain bliss;
And erase from thy heart all sin and sorrow!
Remember the praises of the One Who sustaineth all things
Whose names innumerable millions chant in praise!
The essence of the Vedas, Puranas and Simritis
Is to contemplate the One, the Holy Name.
He who but treasureth the Lord in his heart for a moment,
Who can recount his enrichment or his exaltation?
With those, O Lord, who aspire but to a single glimpse of Thee,
Save me, Nānak crieth, O Lord, with them save me!
In this Song of Peace is the Holy Name
Which, like ambrosia, bestoweth bliss when tasted:
It indwelleth in the hearts of the Lord's saints.

Aṣṭapadī, 1; *Paurī*, 1

---

[1] These four lines refer successively to Guru Nānak, Guru Angad, Guru Amar Das, and Guru Ram Das.

3

prabh kāi simran garbh nā basai

He that remembereth the Lord goes not to the cave of rebirth;
When we remember the Lord, the pang of death departeth:
When we remember the Lord, the fear of death is gone;
When we remember the Lord, our enemies are baffled;
He who remembereth the Lord, no snares are set for him;
Through their remembrance of the Lord
His Saints keep vigil night and day;
Remembering the Lord, no man feeleth fear;
While the Lord is remembered, sorrow troubleth not,
In the company of the Lord's Saints
Men attain to the gift of remembering Him:
Nānak, through the love of God
All life's treasures are obtained.

Aṣṭapadī, 1; *Pauri*, 2

4

prabh kai simran ridh sidh nau nidh

By remembering the Lord we obtain wealth, mystical powers, and the nine treasures:
By remembering the Lord we obtain
Divine knowledge, the gift of meditation, and true wisdom.
To remember God is the real essence
Of every kind of devotion, penance, and prostration.
All delusive awareness of that which seems other than the Lord
Is, on remembering the Lord, dispelled.
To remember the Lord is to bathe in the holy rivers;
To remember the Lord is to be honoured in His Presence;
Who remembers the Lord, his acts are always righteous;
Who remembers the Lord feels His Will to be ever sweet.
In remembering the Lord there is profit.
They remember the Lord whom the Lord hath inspired to remember Him:
Nānak prayeth to be worthy to touch their feet!

Aṣṭapadī, 1; *Pauri*, 3

5
prabh kā simran sabh te ūcā

To remember the Lord is the highest religious duty:
By remembering the Lord many, very many have been saved;
The remembrance of God quencheth the body's desires:
And in the remembrance of the Lord man knoweth all mysteries;
There is no fear of death while one remembers God;
In remembering Him, all wishes are satisfied,
All uncleanness is washed away from the mind,
And His ambrosial Name fills the whole heart.
The Lord dwelleth on the tongue of His Chosen Ones;
Of such servants of God may Nānak be the servant!

Aṣṭapadī, 1; Pauṛi, 4

6
dīn dard dukh bhañjnā

O Thou who destroyest the pain and grief of the wretched,
O Thou who residest in every heart, helper of the forlorn;
I have taken refuge in Thee:
O Lord, be with Nānak!

Aṣṭapadī, 2, Slok

7
chūtat nahī kot lakh bāhī

Where thou couldst not be saved, though thou hadst a million arms,
Even there, the uttering of the Holy Name shall save Thee!
When thy path is beset with snares and barriers
The Name of the Lord will overcome them at once.
Though a man is born and dies and is reborn many times
His soul shall come to its peace through the Holy Name
And its meditation. Much dirt clogs the soul,
No human effort can ever wash it away;
But the Name of God washeth clean from a myriad sins.
Such a Name as this, in thy soul with adoration repeat it:
Nānak, obtain it in the company of the Saints!

Aṣṭapadī, 2; Pauṛi, 3

8

bauh sāstar bauh simrtī pekhe sarb dhaṅdol

Many Shastras, many Simritis have I seen, and carefully searched them—
They are not equal, O Nānak, to the greatness
Of contemplating the Lord's Priceless Name!

Aṣṭapadī, 3; Slok

9

sagal purkh maiṅ purkh pardhān

Among all men that man is foremost
Who in the company of the saints destroys his self-attachment;
He who deemeth himself lowliest of the low
Shall be deemed the highest.
The mind whose humility is the dust under all men's feet
Shall see the Holy Name in all men's hearts.
He who expels malice from his own heart
Finds the whole creation his friend.
To the saint, Nānak, happiness and sorrow are as one;
Such a man is invulnerable to earthly good or evil.

Aṣṭapadī, 3; Pauri, 6

10

sarb dharm meh sreṣṭ dharm

Of all Religions this is the best Religion,
To utter the Holy Name with adoration, and to do good deeds:
Of all rites the holiest rite
Is to cleanse one's soul in the company of the saints:
Of all strivings, the best striving
To meditate on the Name and praise it for ever;
Of all speeches, the ambrosial speech is
To utter aloud, having hearkened to it, God's glory;
Of all shrines, the most sacred shrine,
Nānak, is the heart in which the Lord indwelleth!

Aṣṭapadī, 3; Pauri, 8

11

nirguniār iāniā so prabh sadā samāl

O worthless and ignorant mortal,
Fix thy heart for ever and ever on God;
Remember, O Nānak, the Lord who made thee:
Then, in the end, He will abide with thee!

Aṣṭapadī, 4; Slok, 1

12

ratan tyāg kauḍī sung rucai

Man flingeth away a ruby and hankereth for an empty shell;
He forsaketh truth and yearneth after falsehood.
That which he must part with he thinketh everlasting;
God he thinketh distant, who is eternal;
Man is busy and troubled about what he must abandon;
He forgetteth the Lord who will in the end preserve him,
He washeth away the sandal-paste of the virtues;
Like the donkey, he yearneth to roll in the dust.
The perverse have fallen into the gulf of ignorance:
Nānak prayeth, O Merciful Lord, help them out!

Aṣṭapadī, 4; Pauri, 4

13

tu thākar tum pai ardās

Thou art the Lord; to Thee we pray;
Thou hast given us this living breath and this bodily vessel.
Lord, Thou art Mother and Father, we are Thy children.
By Thy Grace we attain endless happiness:
Who is there that knoweth Thy bounds?
O Lord, Thou art Higher than the highest.
Thou art the Thread on which the whole creation is strung,
And all Thy creation abideth by Thy Will.
And it is Thou alone who knowest Thy Way and Thy Measure:
Nānak, Thy Slave, is ever a sacrifice unto Thee!

Aṣṭapadī, 4; Pauri, 8

14

denhār prabh chod kai

They who abandon God, the Giver of all things,
And who attach themselves to worldly pleasures, they
Shall attain to nothing. Nānak, without the Name
Their honour shall lie in the dust!

Aṣṭapadī, 5; *Slok* .

15

rehat avar kich avar kamāvat

There are those who profess one thing and practise another,
Who talk like devotees, with no love in their hearts:
But the Lord in His Wisdom knoweth all things.
The mere outward garment cannot please Him.
He who preacheth to others what he doth not practise
Shall be born and die again in unending lives.
But he in whose heart the Formless One indwelleth
Shall save the world by his teaching.
Only those, Lord, who have won Thy Love
Have grasped Thee truly:
Nānak is prostrate at the feet of such seers!

Aṣṭapadī, 5; *Pauri*, 7

16

kām krodh ar lobh moh, bins jāe ahimev

O Lord, Nānak hath taken refuge in Thee:
Through Thy Grace, O Divine Guru, drive
Lust, wrath, greed, attachment, self-love, from his heart.

Aṣṭapadī, 6; *Slok*, 1

17

jeh prasād arog kañcan dehi

Fix thy thoughts upon that loving God
By whose grace thy body remains sturdy and hale;

Sing, O soul, His Name and attain bliss
By Whose Mercy thou art saved from dishonour,
Fall, O soul, at the feet of that Good Lord
By whose Favour all thy sins are hidden:
Remember at every breath the Most High God
By Whose Bounty thou transcendest sorrow;
Nānak, serve the Lord with all thy heart
By Whose Goodness thou hast attained the hard-won prize
Of existence in the human body.

Aṣṭapadī, 6; *Pauri*, 3

18

agam agādh parbraham soe

Not to be grasped or sounded is the living God;
He who contemplateth His Name shall be saved.
Listen, O friends, Nānak entreateth ye
To the splendid virtues of living saints.

Aṣṭapadī, 7; *Slok*, 1

19

sādh kai sang na kabhun dhāvai

In the company of the saints
The mind hankereth not wildly;
In the company of the saints
The soul attaineth to happiness;
In the company of the saints
Man glimpseth the invisible;
In the company of the saints
He endureth the unendurable;
In the company of the saints
We reach the heights of the spirit;
In the company of the saints
We enter the Lord's Presence;
In the company of the saints
We acquire all the virtues;

In the company of the saints
We are aware only of God;
In the company of the saints
We are granted His Name, life's treasure;
Nānak is ever a sacrifice
Unto the living saints.
Aṣṭapadī, 7; Pauri, 4

20

man sācā mukh sacā soe

He who is true in heart and speech,
Who seeth none but the One Lord,
Such a one, Nānak, is Brahm-gyānī.[1]
Aṣṭapadī, 8; Slok, 1

21

brahm gyānī sadā nirlep

Who knoweth God liveth ever unattached
Like the lotus unsullied by the pond's water:
Who knoweth God taketh no stain
But, like the sun, warmeth and drieth all things;
Who knoweth God looks on all things with equal eyes
Like the wind that bloweth alike on the rich and poor man;
Who knoweth God is unshakeably long-suffering
Like the ground that one man diggeth, and another smeareth with sandal-paste;
This is the attribute of the knower of God:
His nature is fire-life, all cleansing.
Aṣṭapadī, 8; Pauri, 1

---

[1] Brahm-gyānī is one who has attained perfect knowledge and experience of God. He is a fully God-illumined soul who ever lives in the highest spiritual state. In the eight hymns, to follow, the character, personality and spiritual powers of a Brahm-gyānī are described.

22

brahm-gyānī nirmal te nirmalā

Who knoweth God is, of the pure, the purest,
Like swift-flowing water with which dust cannot mingle;
Light imbueth the mind of the man who knoweth God
Wholly, as the earth is wholly enwrapped by the sky:
To the man who knoweth God, friend and foe are as one:
Who knoweth God is without self-conceit:
Though he is the highest of the high,
Yet he keeps his mind in utter humility—
Nānak, these only are Brahm-gyanis, the Knowers of God,
Whom God Himself in His Grace hath so made.

Aṣṭapadī, 8; *Pauri*, 2

23

brahm-gyānī sagal kī rīnā

Who knoweth God maketh himself the dust under other men's feet,
Who knoweth God attaineth to ecstasy of spirit,
Who knoweth God showereth compassion on all men,
Who knoweth God can do no evil act,
Who knoweth God regardeth all men equally,
From his divine eyes he sheddeth nectar.
Who knoweth God is free from all attachments:
Noble and pure are the paths of the man who knoweth God.
Who knoweth God is nourished by divine knowledge:
Who knoweth God contemplateth none but God.

Aṣṭapadī, 8; *Pauri*, 3

24

brahm-gyānī ek ūpar ās

The man who knoweth God clingeth to God as his only stay,
Who knoweth God suffereth no doom,
Who knoweth God is steeped in humility,

In the man who knoweth God there is a constant urge to goodness.
Who knoweth God hath no worldly entanglements,
Who knoweth God reineth his wandering mind,
Who knoweth God his deeds are godly,
Whatever he doeth beareth excellent fruit.
In the company of the man who knoweth God all shall be saved—
Nānak, the whole world exalteth the man who knoweth God!

Aṣṭapadī, 8; *Pauri*, 4

25

brahm-gyānī kai ekai rang

Who knoweth God dwelleth undisturbed in the love of God,
God abideth eternally with the man who knoweth God,
The Name of God is the stay of the man who knoweth God,
The Name of God is as his household and retinue.
The man who knoweth God is ever wakeful,
The man who knoweth God hath discarded all self-will,
In the mind of the man who knoweth God there is ever delight,
In the heart of the man who knoweth God there is ever happiness.
Who knoweth God abideth in peace and at rest—
O Nānak, death shall not touch the man who knoweth God.

Aṣṭapadī, 8; *Pauri*, 5

26

brahm-gyānī brahm kā betā

The man who knoweth God is called a Brahm-gyānī,
Who knoweth God loveth only the One God,
Who knoweth God is free from all cares,
Pure and true are the thoughts of him who knoweth God,
He becometh a Brahm-gyānī whom God maketh so;
Great is the glory of the Brahm-gyānī,
And only through great good fortune is a meeting with a Brahm-gyānī obtained.

One should make oneself a sacrifice unto the Brahm-gyānī.
Even gods like Siva seek for a Brahm-gyānī:
O Nānak, in the Brahm-gyānī God himself indwelleth.

Aṣṭapadī, 8; *Pauri*, 6

27

brahm-gyānī kī kīmat nāhī

The man who knoweth God cannot have a price set on him,
All that is, dwelleth in the mind of the man who knoweth God,
Who can sound the secret depths of the man who knoweth God!
Hail, eternal hail, unto him, unto him, the Brahm-gyānī!
No words can express the greatness of the Brahm-gyānī
Who knoweth God is the master of all things—
Who can take the measure of the man who knoweth God?
Only the Brahm-gyānī knoweth the excellence of the Brahm-gyānī.
The man who knoweth God is without ends or limits—
Nānak prostrateth himself ever to the man who knoweth God!

Aṣṭapadī, 8; *Pauri*, 7

28

brahm-gyānī sab srist kā kartā

The man who knoweth God is the creator of the universe,
Who knoweth God liveth for ever and dieth not,
Who knoweth God bestoweth goods of the body and spirit,
Who knoweth God is the perfect Lord of life,
Who knoweth God is the stay of the forsaken,
The man who knoweth God extendeth a saving hand over the humanity.
The man who knoweth God hath the world under his control.
Who knoweth God is one with the Formless One.
Only a Brahm-gyānī can acquire the glory of a Brahm-gyānī—
Nānak, the man who knoweth the Lord is himself the Lord of all!

Aṣṭapadī, 8; *Pauri*, 8

29

urdhāre jo antar nām

He who preserveth the Lord's name in his inmost heart,
Who seeth the light of the Lord in all hearts,
And who at every moment prostrateth himself to the Lord,
He is truly an *Aparas*,[1] who will save all men.

Aṣṭapadī, 9; *Slok*, 1

30

mithiā nāhī rasnā paras

Nānak, among millions of men there is scarcely one Aparas
Whose tongue will not touch falsehood,
Whose heart, yearneth for the vision of the Immaculate One,
Whose eyes covet not the beauty of his neighbour's wife,
Who serveth the Lord's Saints and loveth them,
Whose ears will not hear evil spoken against any,
Since in his heart he deemeth himself lowliest of all men,
Who by the Guru's grace has freed himself from all wickedness,
Has banished all evil desires from his heart,
Has conquered the passions, and is free from the five cravings!

Aṣṭapadī, 9; *Pauri*, 1

31

baisno so jis ūpar so prasan

He is a true Vaishnav on whom God's favour hath alighted,
Who dwelleth apart from worldly entanglements
And performeth right actions without seeking a reward for them.
Such a Vaishnav lives a life of true piety:
He seeketh no gain from any good deed he doeth,
But setteth his heart only on the Lord's service and the singing of the Lord's praises;

[1] The Aparas were a sect who prided themselves on never touching coins or anything made of metal.

And with his body and his mind remembereth ever the Lord,
And hath compassion upon all living creatures.
He holdeth fast to the Lord's Name and inspireth others to meditate on it.
Nānak, such a Vaishnav attains to the supreme state.

Aṣṭapadī, 9; *Pauri*, 2

32
prabh kī āgiā ātam hitāvai

He who in his heart ever loveth God's ordinances
Is called a *Jīvan Mukt*, who while still living is saved:
He accepteth joy and sorrow with an equal mind:
He is always happy and never set apart from God.
To him gold and dross are as one,
Nectar and strong poison are as one,
Honour and dishonour are as one,
The king and the beggar are as one.
He who deemeth that what God ordaineth is best
Know him, Nānak, as a *Jīvan Mukt*: who while still alive has found salvation.

Aṣṭapadī, 9; *Pauri* 7

33
ustat kareh anek jan ant nā parāvār

Innumerable are they who sing the praises of the Lord,
To whose glory there is no end, no limit:
Nānak, God hath shaped His Creatures
Of many kinds and endlessly diverse forms!

Aṣṭapadī, 10; *Slok*

34
karn kāran prabh ek hai dūsar nāhī koe

The Maker and Ground of all things is the One Lord.
There is none to set beside Him.
Nānak is ever a Sacrifice unto Him
Who pervadeth sea and land and the sky and the underworld!

Aṣṭapadī, 11; *Slok*, 1

35

sukhī basai maskīnīā āp nivār talai

Those who have destroyed self-will and live in humility,
Those, the meek, are happy. The haughty great
Are consumed, O Nānak, as in a furnace
By the fire of their own pride!

Aṣṭapadī, 12; *Slok*, 1

36

jab lag jānai mujh te kich hoe

There can be no peace for man
So long as he thinketh that of himself he can do anything;
He shall wander from womb to womb in the cycle of births;
So long as he deemeth one man a friend and another an enemy,
So long shall he have no rest for his mind;
So long as man is in love with the illusory goods of the world
So long shall Dharmraj, the Justiciar King, continue to punish him.
It is by God's Grace that man can be freed from bondage;
And by the Guru's grace, saith Nānak, pride and self-will are removed!

Aṣṭapadī, 12; *Pauri*, 4

37

sant saran jo jan parai

He who taketh refuge at the feet of the saints
Hath entered on the path of his salvation:
But he, O Nānak, who vilifieth the saints
Falls into an endless cycle of births.

Aṣṭapadī, 13; *Slok*, 1

38

tajo siānap sur jano simro har har rāe

My friends, discard the devices of worldly wisdom.
Remember only thy Lord, who is the Highest.
Set all thy hopes upon the Lord, saith Nānak:
So shall sorrow, error and fear depart.

Aṣṭapadī, 14; *Slok*, 1

39

jion mandir ko thāmai thaman

Even as a pillar upholdeth a temple-roof
So the word of the Guru is a prop for the mind,
As a stone can float over a river if a boat carrieth it
So mortals are saved from sinking by clinging to the Guru's feet;
As a lamp giveth light in the darkness,
So, on encountering the Guru, there is light in the heart;
As it is for a man when lost in the wilds he suddenly findeth his path
So it shall be, like a sudden light,
When he joineth the congregation of the saints.
I crave for the dust under the feet of such saints:
O God, fulfil the desires of Nānak's heart!

Aṣṭapadī, 15; *Pauri*, 3

40

rūp na rekh nu rang kich

God hath no form, outline, or colour:
He transcendeth these three modes.
O Nānak, He conferreth on those who please Him
The gift of the knowledge of God.

Aṣṭapadī, 16; *Slok*, 1

41

bāraṅ bār bār pradh japīāi

Ever, ever, ever repeat the Name of the Lord:
Satiate thy mind and body by drinking its nectar.
The holy man who hath obtained the jewel of Thy Name
Will look, O Lord, on no other than Thee.
The Divine Name for him is wealth,
It is beauty and it is delight,
The name is his happiness, it is his companion.
He who has been satisfied with the savour of the Name
Shall find his whole body and soul absorbed in it.
To contemplate the Name rising, or resting, or sleeping
Is, O Nānak, the proper task of the man devoted to God!

Aṣṭapadī, 17; *Paurī*, 6

42

satpurkh jin jāniā satgur tis kā nāu

He who knoweth the True Being,
Know him to be the True Guru;
O Nānak, the Guru's disciple is saved by his companionship
And by singing the praises of the Lord!

Aṣṭapadī, 18; *Slok*, 1

43

gur ke greh sevak jo rahai

The disciple who serves at the Guru's feet,
And patiently obeys the Guru's orders,
And has ceased to be full of self-will,
Ever in his heart meditates on the Name,
And abandons his will to the True Guru—
Such a man's doings shall prosper!
He who serves the True Guru without seeking gain for his service,
Such a man shall attain to the Lord.

The servant on whom God showereth grace,
Nānak saith, will acquire wisdom from the Guru.

Aṣṭapadī, 18; *Pauri*, 2

44

sāth nā cālai bin bhajan

O man, nothing shall go with thee from this world,
Except thy devotion to God!
The delights of this world are as dust.
Nānak, true wealth is repeating God's Name!

Aṣṭapadī, 19; *Slok*, 1

45

sang nā cālas terai dhanā

Thy riches will not go with thee:
Why dost thou cling to them so, O fool?
Son, companions, brethren, wife—
Which of these will stand by thee?
Kingdoms, earthly delights, heaps of gold—
Which of these will lead you to deliverance?
Horses, elephants, charioteers
Are a foolish pageantry and a false glory.
The fool forgets who gave him all these things:
Nānak, He forgetteth the Name, and afterwards
    repenteth.

Aṣṭapadī, 19; *Pauri*, 5

46

phirat phirat prabh āio

After wandering and wandering, O Lord,
I have come at last to take refuge in Thee.
Nānak's humble prayer, O God, is—
'Let me be busy in Thy service!'

Aṣṭapadī, 20; *Slok*, 1

47

so kioṅ bisrai jo ghāl nā bhanai

Why forget Him
Who never letteth man's efforts go for nothing.
Why forget Him, who acknowledgeth all service,
Why forget Him, who hath given thee all thou hast,
Why forget Him, who is the life of all things living,
Why forget Him, who preserveth us even in the fire, in the womb?
By the grace of the Guru some rare soul seeth God—
Why forget Him who helps us out of the net of sin
And joins to Him even those who during many births had broken with Him?
The perfect Guru hath taught me this essential truth:
Nānak saith, Lord, Thy servant meditateth on Thee!

Aṣṭapadī, 20; *Pauri*, 4

48

sargun nirgun niraṅkār sun samādhī āp

Manifest in all things, He is also the Unmanifest Ground of all things:
He is Formless: He is Transcendent.
Out of Himself, Nānak, He made all things:
Into Himself all things are again absorbed.

Aṣṭapadī, 21; *Slok*, 1

49

jeh āp racio parpaṅc akhārā

When God made this illusion, the world,
He diffused the three mental states: stupidity, passion and tranquillity.
Good and evil then came to be spoken of,
So did the fear of Hell and the hope of Heaven.
All human temptations and earthly snares,

Self-will, worldly attachment, doubt and fear,
Pain and pleasure, worldly honour and dishonour
Were set moving by God in innumerable shapes.
It is all God's play, and God is the spectator:
When He lets the curtain fall, there is only God.

Aṣṭapadī, 21; *Pauri*, 7

50

jīā jant ke thākarā

O Lord of men and of the creatures,
Thou art present in all things:
O Nānak, One God is all pervading!
Where is there to be seen another?

Aṣṭapadī, 22; *Slok*, 1

51

gyān anjan gur diā

As a salve for our eyes, the Guru hath given us
   Divine knowledge:
By which the darkness of ignorance is dispelled!
By the Grace of God I met the Guru:
And, saith Nanak, my mind is filled with light!

Aṣṭapadī, 23; *Slok*, 1

52

sant janā kā pekhan sabh brahmn

The saint seeth the Light of the Lord in all things:
In the heart of the saint there is nothing but faith,
The saint listeneth only to good words,
His heart is set on the Lord who pervadeth all things.
The code of the saint who knoweth God
Is to speak the truth to all men;
All that cometh to pass he accepteth
As being the Lord's sweet Will.

For He knoweth the Lord as the Ground of all manifestations.
He seeth God in the human heart, and in the world outside man.
Nānak, on beholding the Lord, all men are enchanted!

Aṣṭapadī, 23; Pauri, 4

53

prabh kī ustat karo sant mīt

Exalt the Name of the Lord, O my beloved saints,
With full awareness and single-mindedness!
In these Hymns of Peace there is calm of mind,
There are the Lord's praises, there is His Holy Name!
He who hoardeth the Name in his heart shall be wealthy,
And all his desires shall be fulfilled;
He shall become a man of distinction, world-famous,
He shall obtain the highest spiritual state.
And shall not again endure death and rebirth.
Nānak, he who is blessed by the Lord
Shall depart after earning the wealth of the Name.

Aṣṭapadī, 24; Pauri, 5

54

khem ṣānt ridh sidh nav nidh

Repose, peace, wealth, the nine treasures,
Understanding, divine wisdom, all occult powers,
Knowledge, devotion, union with and meditation on God,
The highest knowledge, the benefits of bathing in holy places,
The four objects of life,[1] the soul's blossoming
As it flowers amid all things and is detached from all things,
Beauty, good sense, grasp of reality
And the power of looking on all things with an equal eye,
These gifts shall be obtained by him who recites the Sukhmanī
And who hearkens inwardly, Nānak saith, to the Name.

Aṣṭapadī, 24; Pauri, 6

[1] The four objects of life are: (1) enjoyment (kama); (2) material interest (arth); (3) ethical living (dharma); (4) spiritual freedom (mokṣā).

55

jis man basai sunai lāe prīt

He in whose heart this Song of Peace indwelleth
Or he who heareth it with loving heart,
In him the Lord's rememberance is awakened,
The pangs of death and new birth are destroyed,
His precious human soul forthwith obtains salvation;
His fame shall be spotless and his speech like nectar:
The Name of God shall now pervade his soul.
Sorrow and sickness, fear and doubt will vanish.
His acts shall be pure; men will call him a saint,
And his life shall be blessed with the highest glory.
Nānak saith: Because of these virtues
This is called Sukhmanī, the Hymns of Peace!

Aṣṭapadī, 24; *Pauri,* 8

II. OTHER HYMNS OF GURU ARJAN

ੴ

1

goel āyā goelī kyā tis danph pasār

Man, thou art a herdsman, pausing at a pastureland:
Why build thyself a grand and showy house,
When thy time is up thou must go hence;
Remember thy true abode.
Man, serve the true Guru,
Sing his praise with devotion,
Why be caught by the emptiness of insignificant things?

Though thou art here like a guest for the night
Who must part betimes in the morning,
Thou makest thyself busy with the world's affairs:
Remember, this is a garden of flowers that must fade.

Why sayest thou: 'This is mine, this is mine?'
Seek the Lord who hath given thee all thou ownest;
In the end thou must needs set on thy way
Leaving thy millions behind thee.

Saith Nānak: After countless births,
Thou hast attained to the prize of human form,
Set now thy thoughts on the Divine Name.
The day of thy summoning is near.

Sri Rag, page 50

2

jā ko muṣkal at banai

When a man is in dire straits
And there come none to help him,
When his enemies press hard on him
And his kinsmen desert him,
When he has lost all hope and help,

Let him only set mind on the Lord
And no harm shall touch him.
The Lord is the strength of the weak,
Unborn, Undying, Eternal,
Through the word of the Guru
Know ye the True Lord.

When a man is weak
With hunger and wretchedness,
Not a penny in his pocket,
No one to give him kind word,
No one to help him in need,
All his work coming to nothing,
Let him only set his mind on the Lord
And he shall obtain a lasting kingdom.

When a householder wrapped in family
Is plagued by worries and by illnesses,
Is sometimes happy, sometimes sad,
Wandering in all directions,
But never peaceful, never at ease in his mind,
Let him only set his mind on the Lord
And both his body and mind will have joyous repose.

When a man has become the slave
Of lust, anger, worldly attachment,
When sordid greed has turned him into a miser,
When he has committed the four major sins[1]
And become a bloody despot,
And though, moreover, he has never given a thought
To holy psalms of scriptures,
Let him only set his mind on the Lord
For one moment with real attention
And his soul shall be set free.

And a man may know by heart,
The four Vedas, the Shastras, the Simritis,

---

[1] The four major sins according to Hindu tradition are: (1) seduction of teacher's wife; (2) killing cows; (3) killing a Brahmin; (4) stealing more than two pounds of gold.

He may perform penances, become an adept in the art of Yoga,
He may visit all the places of pilgrimages,
He may carry out all the rites twice over,
He may prostrate himself in adoration after his ablutions,
But if the love of God is not in that man's soul
To Hell he shall surely go.

And a man may possess lordship over others,
With every pleasure at command,
He has beautiful gardens to revel in, he speaks and he is obeyed;
And his whole life may be passed in various enjoyments,
Yet if such a man remember not the Highest,
He shall die and be reborn as a crawling reptile.

And a man may be rich, a gentleman of repute and impeccable manners;
He may honour his father and mother, love his brothers and friends;
He may have armies at command and all may honour him,
Yet if such a man remember not his God
Hell shall be his portion.

Or another man has a body without flaw and sickness,
He has never encountered sorrow and anguish,
He has never been troubled by the thought of death.
Night and day he gives to pleasure.
Everything he takes as his own,
And his conscience never pricks him.
Yet if such a man remember not the Lord,
He shall be victim of death's demons.

The man on whom God showers mercy
Enters into the company of the Lord's saints,
The more he frequents the company of the saints
The deeper grows his love for the Lord.
Our Lord is the Lord of both the worlds,
He is our only stronghold.
When the true Lord is pleased, saith Nānak,
The Divine Name is attained.

Sri Rag, page 70

3

khojat khojat darsan cāhe

Dark wood after dark wood I have groped through,
In my longing, O Lord, to behold Thee,
Is there anyone who will make me one with the Lord,
Who is both the unmanifest and the manifest?

One may know by heart and give lectures on the six Hindu Systems;
One may have mastered all the liturgies,
Have the proper caste-mark on one's forehead,
Have bathed at all the places of pilgrimages,
Be a yogi adept in yogic feats and postures,
And yet not so will one attain the peace of mind.

For years one may practise austerities,
And repeat holy words,
And wander all over the world
Yet though one is such a Yogi,
One's mind will remain restless
Not for one moment will it attain peace.

But God in His mercy
Has made me encounter a Saint.
My mind and body are joyous;
There is peace established within me.
The Immortal Lord now in my heart indwelleth,
Nānak singeth the songs of the Lord's glory.

Rag Majh, page 98

4

sabh kich ghar mai bāhar nāhī

Everything is within oneself, nothing outside oneself,
He who seeketh the Lord outside Himself is lost in doubt;
He who by the Guru's grace hath attained to God within himself,
Is happy in himself, and in the world beyond him is happy.

Jhim, Jhim, the nectar falls like rain within him,
The mind drinketh it and hearkens to and contemplates the Word.
Day and night it rejoiceth
And it sporteth ever with God.

Separated from God through many deaths and births,
I have now met Him and I by the Guru's grace,
Though I was as the dry tree, am now green again.

Having encountered the Guru,
I have attained to wisdom
And I contemplate the Name
As waves blend with water,
So my light is blended with the Lord's Light.
Saith Nānak: The doors of delusion have been destroyed
No longer shall the soul wander or be separated from Thee.

Rag Majh, page 102

5

tū merā pitā tū hai merā mātā

Thou art my father,
Thou art my mother,
Thou art my brother,
Thou art my kin,
In all places Thou art my Saviour,
What should I fear and why should I repine?

Through Thy grace
Have I grasped Thee,
Thou art my covert,
Thou art my pride,
There is none beside Thee.
The whole Universe is the field of Thy sport.

Thou hast created all creatures big and small,
To each allotted his task
According to Thy Will.

All that is done is Thy doing,
There is naught that we can do.

Meditating on Thy Name
I attain the height of happiness;
Exalting Thee in Song
I am brimmed full of bliss.
By the grace of the perfect Guru
My heart is made full of rejoicings
Saith Nānak, and Victory has been won.

Rag Majh, page 103

6

BĀRĀMĀHĀ MĀJH

(i)

kirt karm ke vīchde

We are set apart from Thee,
Because of our own past deeds;
Lord, through Thine unbounded mercy
Make us again one with Thee.
Weary of wandering endlessly:
North, south, east, west
We have come, Lord, to take refuge in Thee.
A cow that gives no milk is useless.
Unless a plant has water, it shrivels and bears no fruit,
Unless man meets his Friend and Master.
The home, the husband comes not to,
That home is like a burning furnace,
All ornamentation, all smearing of the lips with betel,
Like the body itself are short lived.
Unless the Beloved Friend dwells within us,
Our companions and our dear ones are like demons;
Nānak thus prayeth:
Lord, through Thy mercy, grant me Thy holy Name;
Unto me with my Beloved Friend whose home is eternal.

(ii)

sāvaṇ sarsī kāmṇī

It is the rainy month of Sāvan,
The hearts of those brides
That love His lotus feet have blossomed,
The light of Truth has been infused
Into their bodies and minds;
They are nourished only by the Holy Name,
All earthly joys are of a fading colour;
They pass, they become dust;
But nectar is drunk by those
Whom the man of God inspires;
The trees and even the humble herbs of the fields
Are freshened by the rain of the Lord's love,
Who is Infinite and all-powerful.
My soul yearneth to meet the Lord,
Through Grace He can be met.
And, O Friend, may I be a sacrifice
Ever unto him who hath attained the Lord.
Saith Nānak, When God showeth grace
He can be grasped through the Word.
The rainy month of Sāvan is a delight to the brides,
Within whose hearts the Holy Name indwelleth.

Rag Majh, page 133

7

vade vade jo dīsai log

Those who appear great men in the world's eyes
Have a life ever cankered with anxious care;
Who can be truly great for his wealth alone?
He is great who single-mindedly loves the Lord.

The land owners are always fighting for more land,
Their thirst is unquenched till it is time to leave and go,
Nānak saith: The heart of the matter is,
Without fixing the mind on God, there is no salvation.

Rāg Gauri, page 188

8

karai duhkarm dikhāvai hor

Though a man on earth do evil deeds
And outwardly seem virtuous
In God's Court he shall be handcuffed like a thief;
He is truly the Lord's man,
Who remembers Him all the time;
The one Lord pervades the earth, the sea and the sky,
The Lord's is the one moving spirit.

He who with venom in his heart
Speaketh in honeyed words,
In Yama's court he shall be bound
And beaten for his hypocrisy.

The hypocrite sins in various ways,
But always sins secretly;
Yet in an instant his guile
Shall be made known to the world.

Saith Nānak: That man in whose heart Truth indwelleth,
Is as a man made drunk with the Divine Name,
He is blessed with the Grace of God.

Rag Gauri, page 194

9

jab eh man mai kari gumānā

When a man's mind entertains vanity,
His self-conceit makes him mad; He wanders in error.
When he thinks himself as the dust under anyone's feet,
Then he beholds the Lord in every one,
The fruit of humility is unforced joy:
This is the gift the Guru has bestowed on me.

When a man judges his neighbour to be evil,
He is himself the victim of evil thoughts.
When he discards the distinction of 'mine' and 'thine'
No man is then his enemy.

When a man clamours: 'It is mine, it is mine'.
Then he is in the midst of many troubles.
When he recognizes the Supreme Giver and Doer,
Then he is free from pain and free from sorrow.

When a man binds himself to worldly attachments,
He is caught up in the endless cycles of deaths and rebirths;
When all his worldly delusions are dissipated,
He attains to oneness with God.
When a man considers his selfhood as separate from God's,
He suffers agony and grief. Should he recognize the One Spirit;
Then he has grasped the Ground of all Manifestation.

The hunger for worldly wealth is never satisfied,
The world's thirst is not quenched;
But let a man detach himself from worldly attachments,
And after his trial he shall prosper.
When through the Lord's Infinite Mercy in the mind's temple
I encountered the True Guru,
The lamp of wisdom was lighted.
I understood then what victory and defeat are,
I grasped life's purpose.

The One Lord is the Cause of all causes,
Knowledge, wisdom, discrimination are His gifts to us;
He is not far, He is near, He is with us all.
Saith Nānak: Praise the Lord with an abiding love for Him!

Rag Gauri, page 235

10

BĀVAN AKHARĪ

(i)

at sunder kulīn catur mukh gyānī

However handsome, well-born, wise,
Clever in speech and wealthy,
He is no more than a corpse, sayeth Nānak;
If the love of God is not in his heart.

(ii)

lekhai kade na chutīai

By merit alone, of our deeds,
We could never be liberated, O Lord,
Every moment we err and sin.
O Saviour True, save us through Thy mercy,
Says Nānak, and take us across the fearful ocean of life.

Rag Gauri, page 253, verses 16 and 52

11

rakhe rakhanhar āp ubārian

Our Saviour saveth: it is our Redeemer who hath saved us;
At the feet of the Guru, all deeds become fruitful;
When the Lord showereth His Grace upon us
We do not forget Him;
We cross life's terrifying ocean
In the holy company of the saints.
In an instant God shall destroy
The slanderers, the perverse, the wicked.
Nānak, have faith in the Lord only, as the prop of life;
In the contemplation of the Lord
There is joy newborn and all old sorrows vanish.

Rag Gujri, Var, page 517

12

vadh sukh rainaḍīai

O peace-giving night, prolong thyself,
For I am in love with my Lord;
O wretched sleep shorten thyself,
That I may always clasp His feet.
I long for the dust of His feet,
And I crave for the Holy Name of the Lord,
For the love of which I have given up the world;
Forsaking all my evil ways.

I have become drenched in the love of my Belovéd
And I am intoxicated with His Spirit.
I have encountered my Beloved on the True Path;
He hath taken me by the arm and I am lost in His love.
Nānak imploreth Thee, Lord,
To extend to him this favour,
That he may continue to cling to Thy feet.

O my friends and companions,
Let us devote ourselves to the Lord's Feet;
In our hearts is a deep-seated devotion to the Beloved;
Let us pray that we may continue to serve Him.
Let us meditate on the Lord and let us meet His saints,
And it shall be granted to us to serve Him.
Let us forsake the sins of vanity and attachment,
And dedicate to Him our bodies, our souls, our wealth.
The Lord is great, all pervasive and perfect
On meeting Him delusion and fear depart.
Nānak supplicateth: O my sister, hear me,
Let us repeat again and again the Divine Name.

The spouse of the Lord is a happy spouse,
And enjoyeth every pleasure;
She shall not become a widow; her Lord is immortal;
No sorrow can touch her as she contemplateth her Master;
Blessed and fortunate is such a woman.
She sleepeth in peace and loseth all her sins;
She awaketh to new delight and to love of the Name.
She remaineth absorbed in the Lord's love,
She weareth the Divine Name as her jewels;
The words of the Beloved sound sweet in her ears.
Nānak proclaimeth: The desires of my heart are fulfilled
I have met the Lord who liveth for ever.
In his heart arise,
Millions of songs of rejoicing;
In whose soul and body
The Lord, the Primal Joy, indwelleth.
The Lord, my Beloved hath no bounds,
Is compassionate, all wealth is His,
He sustaineth the world, He saveth sinners.

The Lord, the Extender of Mercy,
Is He who helpeth us over the terrible ocean.
The Lord extendeth His favour
To those who seek His protection.
Nānak proclaimeth: I have found the Lord, my Beloved,
And He sporteth with me for ever.

Rag Bihagra, page 544

13

ek pitā ekas ke ham bārak

The One God is the Father of all
We are all His children;
O Guru, O Friend, I dedicate my heart to Thee,
If thou lettest me but have a glimpse of God.

I shall touch thy feet,
I shall wash them,
I will give all my heart to Thee,
Hearken, my friend, I have taken refuge in thee,
Teach me how to be one with the Lord.

Free thyself of pride, take refuge in Him,
Accept with joy what He doeth;
Hearken, my friend,
Give thy body, thy mind, thy whole self unto Him
And thus have glimpse of the Divine.

By my Lord's blessing,
By the grace of Saints,
The Divine Name is sweet to me,
The Guru hath been merciful to his slave Nānak.

Rag Sorath, page 611

14

garībī gadā hamāri

Humility is our spiked mace:
To be the dust under everyone's feet

Is my double-edged dagger,
None of the wicked can withstand these weapons.
The Perfect Guru has taught me this.
The Holy Name is the refuge of the Saints.
He who contemplates the Name is liberated:
Millions have been thus set free.

In the company of the Saints
I sing of the Lord's Glory.
I have acquired this Divine Treasure
That is beyond all price.
Saith Nānak: When we lose all awareness of the little, separate self
We see the Divine Supremacy all-pervasive.

Rag Sorath, page 628

15

aukhī ghaḍī nā dekhan deī

Lord, Thou lettest not Thy servants
Face the difficult hour; that is Thy way.
Thy Hand is over Thy Saints to protect them
At every moment of life.
My heart is the Lord's Glory unto the Beloved friend
Who standeth beside me from life's beginning to its end!

Seeing the Lord's exceeding Greatness,
My heart rejoiceth exceedingly.
Saith Nānak: The Lord hath fully protected mine honour.
Contemplate the Lord for ever, and live in bliss.

Rag Dhanasri, page 682

16

jioṅ machlī bin pānīai

As a fish cannot live out of water,
As the thirst of the chātrik
Can be quenched only by the raindrop,

As enchanted by the drum-beat
The deer cometh running to the hunter,
As the honey bee yearneth for the flower
Which on closing entraps it.
With a like intensity the Saints yearn for the Lord:
Only the sight of Him can sate their thirst for him.

Rag Jaitsiri, Var, page 708

17

māṅgoṅ dān thākar nām

I crave from Thee, Lord, the gift of Thy Name,
Nothing else will abide with me.
Through Thy Grace, grant me the singing of Thy Praise,
Kingdoms, gold, sensual delights
Vanish like the shadow cast by a tree.
The man who pursues shadows pursues vanities.

I crave for nothing but God.
All else is illusion:
Saith Nānak, I crave for the dust of the feet of the Saints
On which I will stay my mind.

Rag Todi, page 713

18

bājīgar jaisai bajī pāe

As an actor in a play appears in many guises
So God when His play is ended abandons the guise
And appears as the One only.

What was the shape that appeared and was made to disappear?
Whence did it come and whither did it go?
Out of the Ocean many a wave arises:
Out of Gold are made many kinds of ornaments.
He soweth His manifold seeds, and the fruit ripens;
In the ripe fruit is the same seed again.

A hundred shining vessels
Reflect the same bright sky,
They shall be broken and the sky remain.
Error is caused by greed,
By attachment to the world of illusion.
When we slough off error,
We grasp the One True God.

The soul is eternal and cannot be destroyed.
It is neither born nor does it die.
The Perfect Guru has removed
The filth of attachment to my petty selfhood,
Saith Nānak, and I have reached the heights!

Rag Suhi, page 736

19

darṣān dekh jīvan gur terā

When I see my Beloved Guru, I live;
I have accomplished my task and found my God,
O Lord, grant this prayer only:
Let me follow Thee and grant me Thy Name.
O Beloved Lord, by the grace of the Guru
Keep me in Thy Stronghold.
Few are those who through the Guru's grace reach to Thee.
My Beloved Lord and Friend, hear my prayer.
May my inner heart behold Thy Lotus Feet:
Nānak maketh but one prayer:
May I never forget Thee, Perfect One. Thou art the cradle of virtues.

Rag Suhi, page 741

20

bhalī suhāvī chāprī

Blessed beautiful is the Hut
Where the Lord's praise is sung:
Worthless is the palace
Where the Lord is forgotten.

Poverty is bliss
If it remembereth God
In the holy congregation.
May such worldly greatness be consumed in fire
When it maketh itself Mammon's slave.

To live by grinding corn,
Wearing only a blanket
But having a contented heart,
Is better than ruling a kingdom
Without inner peace.

The man who has nothing to cover his nakedness,
But who walks in the love of God,
Will win honour and courtesy:
But silk attire is worthless
When it increaseth greed.

All things, Lord, are at Thy disposal,
Thou art the Cause of all things
And of all human actions:
Nānak craveth this gift, O Lord,
That with every breath he may remember Thee!

Rag Suhi, page 745

21

abcal nagar gobiṅd gūrū kā

Eternal is the City of my God-like Guru
Wherein souls attain to bliss.
Whoever meditates on His Holy Name
Finds peace here,
For the Lord Himself founded the City.
All that the heart yearneth for is here found:
The Lord Himself certainly hath found it.
Here sons, brothers, disciples are all happy
Singing the praises of their Perfect Lord.
Their labours have been bounteously rewarded.
God is our Lord, He is our Saviour,
Our true Father and Mother.

Nānak saith: May I be as a sacrifice to the Guru
Who hath shed such beauty on this place!

Mansions, homes and booths
Are all lovely
Wherein is heard the Name of the Lord.
The holy and the wise propitiate Him
And Yama's noose is destroyed.
O contemplate the Holy Name,
And Death's noose is destroyed!
Their worship is thus complete, they have their heart's desire,
And the noble-hearted Saints revel in their peace:
Pain, suffering, doubt and delusion have departed.
The True Guru makes perfect through the Word;
Nānak is ever a sacrifice unto Him.

The Lord hath bestowed bountifully, His gift ever increaseth:
Great and glorious is He who since the world's creation
Hath made the Saints His own in every age and protected them.
And shows his mercy on man.
All living creatures dwell in peace in the Lord's city,
It is the Lord that sustaineth them all.

His glory spreadeth on all sides, there is no telling His Greatness.
Nānak saith: I am a sacrifice unto the True Guru
Who hath laid the Eternal Foundation.

In the Lord's city the sermons of Divine Wisdom are being preached and listened to eternally;
The folk contemplate the Lord and His Wisdom,
The Lord as Destroyer of Fear ever sporteth there
And the Unstruck Music is heard.
In the resonance of unstruck melody
The Lord's Saints discourse with each other,
Meditate on the Name and cleanse their souls.
They are set free from the cycle of births, deaths, and rebirths.
Nānak hath found the Guru, hath found God
By whose grace all yearnings are quieted.

Rag Suhi, page 783

22

mohan niṅd nā āvai

O my Beloved, sleep hath fled from me.
I lie awake and I sigh for Thee,
I have adorned myself with necklaces and ornaments,
Garments of fine cloth, collyrium in my eyes,
I waited and longed, longed and waited. When will
   He come home?
I took refuge with the Saints
And prostrated myself at their feet:
'O Saints, unite me with my Beloved,
Unite me with my Life's Jewel,
O when will He come to me?'

Listen, O Friend:
This is the path to Union:
Destroy sense of self,
Thou shalt find then
My Lord within Thee.

Then sing songs of praise and joy
 And meditate on the Blissful one.
Saith Nānak: 'The Lord entered my heart,
I have found the Jewel of Life,
The Beloved hath shown me His Face.
Now I can turn and sleep.
My desires are appeased, peace holds me.
The tale of the Beloved is sweet.
I have found Him, my lost Jewel!'

Rag Bilawal, page 830

23

koi bole rām rām, koi khudā

Some call on the Lord, 'Ram, Ram!' Some cry, 'Khuda!'
Some bow to Him as Gosaīn, some as Allah:
He is called the Ground of Grounds and also the Bountiful,
He is called Kirpādhar and Rahim:
The Mountain of Mercies, the Merciful.

The Hindus bathe in holy waters for His sake;
The Moslems make the pilgrimage to Mecca.
The Hindus worship in temples, the Moslems go down on their mats.
There are those who read the Vedas and those others,
Christians, Jews, Muslims, who read the Semitic scriptures.
Some wear blue, some white robes,
Some call themselves Muslims, some Hindus:
Some aspire to Bahishat, some to Swarga:
The paradises of the Moslems and Hindus.
But Nānak saith: He that knoweth the will of the Lord
He will find out the Lord's secrets!

Rag Ramkalī, page 885

24

androṅ anāh, bahroṅ anāh

That man is blind within and blind without,
Though he pretendeth to sing of the Lord
And performeth ritual washings and puts on caste-marks,
If in his heart he runneth after Mammon.
He cannot remove his inner dirt of self sense.
In births he comes and goes,
Overwhelmed by sleep, played by lust,
And uttereth the name of God.
Though he call himself a Vaishnav,
Since self-will is the goad of his actions
What can he hope to gain?
Pretended holiness is like thrashing empty husks,
Or like the crane who sets among the swans,
Is still on the watch for fish. The swans find him an intruder.
They live upon pearls and precious stones, the crane on frogs,
And finally the poor crane flies away
In fear that the swans might spot his true nature.
Men do as God wills. Why should we blame anyone
When anything happens, God wills that it should?
The True Guru is an ocean-wide lake of pearls:
The sincere seeker after his pearls shall find them.
The True Guru is the holy lake of Mansrover,
And his Sikhs are there gathered like his swans.

The lake is full of pearls and precious stones;
However many the swans eat, they will not be exhausted.
The Sikhs are like swans who remain at the lake for ever
And banquet for ever on jewels. God has so willed it.
Nānak, blessed is the disciple who comes to the Guru:
The Guru will save him, save his family,
Nay, in the end he will save the whole world!

Rag Ramkalī, Var, page 960

25

phuto aṅdā bharam kā

The shell of the egg of delusion has burst.
Light breaks in on the mind, the Guru
Has broken the fetters of the captive soul.
The cycle of births and deaths have ceased
The cauldron of desires bubbles no more
The Guru has given us the Divine Name to cool it.
My enemies, the senses, that assailed me
Have left since I found the Saint's company;
The Lord, who put temptations once in my way,
Now in His Mercy removeth them. What will Death do
Now that I have been released from the burden of my past actions.
I act now without any desire for reward:
From the depths of the ocean I have reached the shore.
The Guru hath done this act of mercy:
Now Truth is my place, my seat, my purpose,
It is Truth, saith Nānak, that I heard and Truth that I trade in and have found Truth within me.

Rag Maru, page 1002

26

cāṅdana cāṅdan āṅgan

Of all the lights in the courtyard
The best light is the light of God in the heart!

Of all the contemplations of the human mind
The best contemplation is the contemplation
Of the Lord's Holy Name;
Of all renunciation
The best renunciation is the renunciation
Of lust, of anger, and of greed;

Of all prayers of the heart
The best prayer is the prayer
To the Guru to be given the Grace
Of properly praising the Lord;

And of all strenuous vigils
The best vigil is a vigil
Spent singing Divine Songs.

Of all man's attachments
The best attachment is the attachment
Of man's heart to the feet of the Lord.

Blessed is he, saith Nānak,
Who is taught such a path and walks on it.
If a man but maketh God his stronghold
All that he does is the best.

Rag Maru, page 1018

27

birkhai heth sabh jant ikathe

At sunset the birds gather in the branches,
Some chirp shrilly, some sing sweetly.
At sunrise again they fly away.
When our time comes, we shall also have to depart.

Sinners are indeed lost. When Azrail gets them
They suffer untold torments, they are flung into hell,
Where Dharmraj, like a usurer, makes them cast up their accounts.

No brother or sister goes with them to Death's kingdom.
They leave behind property, youth, wealth.

Because in their lifetimes they did not know their Lord,
The Ground of Grounds, the Fountain of Mercy,
Now they suffer the agonies of sesame seeds,
Crushed in the mill without mercy for oil.

A man may easily grasp what belongs to another,
But God is near and misses nothing.
The sinner falls into the pit he himself digs:
Greed makes him blind to the future.

He is caught up in births and deaths, and in the cycle he
   suffers:
While he is blind and knows not the Lord
Who is the source of his being
He must suffer pain.

Forgetting God, the sinner walks in the mazes
Of error, caught up in worldly attachments,
Sometimes sad, sometimes happy. He did not encounter the
   Saints
To learn from them the lessons of faith and forbearance.
He suffers from his own selfhood.

It is all God's game:
Some reach the shore, some are drowned in life's terrible
   ocean.
Each man dances as the Lord maketh him dance:
Each man must pay in suffering for bad deeds.

If the Lord showereth His grace,
Upon the Lord I shall meditate,
How by the companionship of the Saints
All men may be saved from Hell.
Give me, O Lord, Thy ambrosial Name as a gift:
So that for ever I may sing Thy Praises.

Rag Maru, page 1019

allāh agam khudāī bande

Allah's depths are not to be sounded, O Ye who plumb for God!
Renounce all worldly attachments. Be as the dust
Under the feet of the Saints, be as a wayfarer:
Such an austere dervish will be pleasing to God!

Let Truth be your prayer, Faith your prayer-mat.
Control your desires; root out vain yearnings:
Make your body a Mosque, your mind its Mullah.

And remembrance of God be your Kalmā: the opening lines of
   your creed:
Let good conduct be your law and your Prophets;
Let your observances and dogmas be renunciation.
Seek most to know how to control the mind,
Search for truth, get life everlasting.

Practise in your heart the Korānic or other teachings
By tethering the straying senses. Set chains of faith
On the five great vices, and earn the gift of charity, contentment
And being acceptable to the Lord.

Let Mercy be your Mecca:
Instead of fasts, use humility:
Seek no other paradise than abiding by the word of your Guru;
For houris, seek in your paradise
The fragrance of the Light
That streameth from the Lord:
Seek no other palace or pleasance than devotion to God.

To practise Truth is to be a Qazi,
To purify the heart is to be a Haji,
To shame the devil is to be a Mullah,
To praise God is to be a Dervish.

Let your praying-hour be at no set time, but all times;
Let your constant prayer be remembrance of God in the heart;

198

Use meditation instead of rosary:
And instead of circumcision
Let chastity check your desires.

Know that all these outward forms are transient,
Are entanglements, like other worldly ties.
All the Mīrs and the Maliks are sold to death:
Only God's Kingdom lasteth

Let your first prayer be God's Praises,
Your second inner peace,
Your third humility, your fourth charity,
Your fifth subduing the five senses to God:
These five prayers will lead you to God's Infinity.

While you live, remember God:
Instead of washing your hands before prayer
Get rid of your evil deeds:
Instead of having a special horn to call for prayer
Grasp, with a pure heart, the Oneness of God.

Eat what you have lawfully earned:
And wash all dirt,
In the river of your heart.
He who follows the Pir
Will indeed go to Paradise
And not be tormented by Azrail.

Discipline your body to virtuous deeds!
Take abiding faith as your spouse
And divine knowledge as your handmaid;
Let purifying the impure be your holy Hadith,
And complete integrity be your turban;
A true Muslim should be tender-hearted
And wash the impurities in his heart.
Not caught in the snare of pleasure, he should be as pure
As flowers, as silk, as clarified butter, as the soft skin of a deer.

He whom the Kindly Lord in His Grace blesseth
Is indeed one real man and Valiant,

Truly a Sheikh, a Haji, one of the faithful:
He on whom the Lord looks with Grace
Is truly the Lord's Servant.

Know ye and grasp ye the Lord,
The Cause of Causes, the Bounteous,
All-loving, All-Good, a Fountain of Mercies
Whose Ordinances are Just and Eternal:
Know him, Nānak saith, and be set free!

Rag Maru, 1083

29

pehloṅ marn kabul kar

Accept first to die,
Abandon hope of living,
Be the dust under the feet of all,
Then come to me.

Rag Maru, Var, page 1103

30

vart nā rahoṅ nāmah ramdānā

I neither keep the Hindu fasts nor the Muslim Ramadan.
I serve Him alone who in the end will save me.
My Lord is both the Muslim Allah and the Hindu Gosain,
And thus have I settled the dispute between the Hindu and the Muslim.
I do not go on the pilgrimage to Mecca
Nor bathe myself at the Hindu holy places.
I serve the One Lord, and none beside Him;
Neither performing Hindu worship nor offering Muslim prayer,
To the Formless One I bow in my heart,
Neither am I a Hindu nor am I Moslem.
Though I belong body and soul to the One God
Who is both Allah and Ram, Listen, O Kabir:
Encountering the True Guru, One encounters God.

Rag Bhairon, page 1136

31

thākar tum sarnāi āyā

O Lord, in Thee I have taken refuge:
Since I have seen Thee, I have no more doubts.
Without my speaking it, Thou knewest my sorrow.
Thou didst cause me to meditate on Thy Name.
My sorrow is gone. I have attained the bliss of oneness with Thee
Through singing Thy praises.
Holding me by the arm, Thou hast guided me out of Maya's
Blind maze and the trap of my worldly attachments.
Nānak saith: The Guru hath broken my fetters;
I who was separated am united with the Lord.

Rag Sarang, page 1218

32

pothī parmesar kā than

In this Holy Book: the Ādi Granth
Resideth the Lord.
Those who sing His praises
In the company of Saints
Attain Divine knowledge.
For this Divine knowledge
Seers and sages thirst,
But few attain concentration on Him;
On whom the Lord is merciful
His desires are fulfilled;
He in whose heart resides the destroyer of fear
Is known in the whole world.
Nānak begs this gift of Thee
May I never forget Thee O Lord.

Rag Sarang, page 1226

33

sainā sādh samūh

Invincible is the army of the Saints.
Great warriors are they; humility is their breast-plate;
The songs of the Lord's Glory are their weapons;
The word of the Guru is their buckler.
They ride the horses, chariots, and elephants
Of the understanding of the Divine Path.
Without fear, they advance towards the enemy.
They ride into battle singing the Lord's praise.
By conquering those five robber chiefs, the senses,
They find they have also conquered the whole world.

Slok Sehskriti, 29; page 1356

34

he kāmaṅ nark bisrāmaṅ

Lust, thou native of hell,
That goadest man into the cycle of births,
Enchanter of hearts, wielding power on the earth and below and above it,
Thou who destroyeth meditation, austerity, and virtue,
And offerest in return but a petty and a passing delight,
Thou who lordest it over high and low,
In the company of the holy, men lose their fear of Thee:
I seek the Lord as a stronghold, saith Nānak.

Slok Sehskriti, 46; page 1358

35

he kal mūl krodhaṅ

Wrath, pitiless, and seed of strife,
Thou enthrallest even the great, and they dance like monkeys.
And in Yama's kingdom the devils punish them.

To frequent thee depraveth man. Nānak saith:
The Lord only, who disperseth the woes of the humble,
Who is ever Merciful, can protect men from thee.

Slok Sehskriti, 47; page 1358

36

he lobha lampat sang sirmorah

O Covetousness, misled by thee
Even the noble are swept away,
By the many winds of greed:
The mind hankers multifariously,
Is unstable, vacillates,
And is not checked by Conscience.
Even before his father and mother,
Friends, kin, dear ones, near ones,
Thou makest man to do what he should not:
Thou makest man eat what should not be eaten:
Thou makest man build what should not be built.
Save, O save me, Lord, in Thy Stronghold,
Save me, saith Nānak: save, save!

Slok Sehskriti, 48; page 1358

37

he junam maran mūlaṅ ahamkāraṅ

O Self-love, Self-will, thou root of births and deaths,
Thou soul of sin, thou makest a man to
Estrange friends and increase the enmity of enemies:
He thinketh ever of heaping up more wealth,
And his soul exhausts itself in deaths and rebirths
And suffers uncountable delights and agonies.
Thou makest man to lose himself in error's dark wood,
And thou strikest him mortally sick with covetousness.

The Lord, O stricken man, is the only physician:
Nānak saith: Meditate the Holy Name!

38

supne ubhī bhaī

In a dream, I was lifted high towards Him,
Why, then, did I not grasp at the hem of His Garments?
My mind bewitched by the Lovely Light that shineth from Him,
I seek for his track. Say, where can I sight it?
What can I do, Sweet Sister my Soul,
That I may meet my Beloved?

Phunhe, 13; page 1362

HYMNS OF GURU TEGH BAHADUR
(1621-1675)

Tegh Bahadur was the youngest son of the warrior Guru Hargobind. He lived a life of contemplative seclusion until he was called upon to assume the leadership of the Sikhs.

He lived mainly in the East of India. He strove against Aurangzeb's challenge to exterminate all religions but his own, and went to meet the Emperor to convince him of his wrong policy. He was publicly beheaded in Delhi on the 11th of November 1675.

One hundred and fifteen hymns by Tegh Bahadur were inserted in the Adi Granth by his son, Gobind Singh, when the latter edited the definitive text of the Holy Book in the year 1705.

1

sādho man kā mān tiāgo

Ye, who seek after Truth, cast down your vanity!
Lust and wrath are wasteful companions. Flee them
By night, by day! Only that spirit is wakeful
That with an equal mind confronts happiness and suffering,
Glory and shame, that regards joy with as much detachment
As pain, as sorrow! that is indifferent to praise,
That is indifferent even to blame, the world's blame,
And that seeks the blissful Nirvāṇā. Nānak,
That seeking is the hardest of all games:
Only the rare Enlightened Ones master it.

Rag Gauri, page 219

2

jagat mai jhuṭhi dekhi prīt

I have found out the falseness of all world attachments.
Everyone seeks his own happiness, One's wife or one's closest friend
Claims, 'He is mine, he is mine!' In life they all cling to one:
But in death neither friend nor wife keep company.
Such are the world's strange ways; I have often taught thee this.
But, my foolish mind, thou hast grasped not my teachings till now!
Saith Nānak: Only by singing the songs of the Lord
Can the pilgrim safely cross life's terrible ocean!

Rag Devghandgari, page 536

3

man re gehio na gur updesā

O soul thou dost not abide by the Guru's teachings.
What can it profit thee
That thou art a clean-shaven anchorite,

Thy garments dyed with ochre?
Thou livest apart from Truth;
Thou squanderest thy life;
Thou art a deceiver
Only that thou mayest feed fully
And sink into bovine slumber;
Thou hast never sought
The roads of devotion
That lead to the Lord.
Thou has lost thy soul
To this world's idols: thou hast forgotten,
O madman, the world's gem, the Name of the Lord,
Thou thinkest of the Lord never:
Thy precious life drains wastefully away.
Man, saith Nānak, wanders ever in error:
Let me think, Lord, only of Thy forgiving Grace!

Rag Sorath, page 633

4

jo nar dukh mai dukh nahī mānai

That man who in the midst of grief is free from grieving,
And free from fear, and free from the snare of delight,
Nor is covetous of gold that he knows to be dust,
Who is neither a backbiter nor a flatterer,
Nor has greed in his heart, nor vanity, nor any worldly attachment,
Who remains at his centre unmoved by good and ill fortune,
Who is indifferent to the world's praise and blame
And discards every wishful fantasy
Accepting his lot in a disinterested fashion,
Not worked upon by lust or by wrath,
In such a man God dwelleth.
The man on whom the Grace of the Guru alights
Understands the way of conduct:
His soul, O Nānak, is mingled with the Lord
As water mingles with water!

Rag Sorath, page 633

5

teh jogī ko jugat na jāno

If his inner self is full of low cravings,
If the greed and the glory of the world still delude him,
There is an art the yogi has not learned:
It is the art of living.
The true yogi dwelleth apart
From the world's delusive praise, its delusive blame:
He dwells where cheap iron and glittering gold
Have the same value; at his centre he is unmoved
By good and by ill fortune, by joy and sorrow.
The restless mind drifts shilly-shally
In all directions, without goal or aim,
One must learn to check and to direct it.
Saith Nānak: He who has learned to master the mind
Is among the liberated, is among the saints!

Rag Dhanāsari, page 685

6

gun gobind gāio nahī, janam akārath kīn

I have never properly sung the praise of the Lord:
Unreal and useless have been all my earthly days.
Saith Nānak: O mind, dive into the love of God
As a fish longs to dive into the Water.

Slok, 1; page 1426

7

patit udhāran bhai haran har anāth ke nāth

From sin, He is the Redeemer;
Of dread, He is the Dispeller;
Of the lost, He is the Guide.
Saith Nānak: Hold this thought in thy mind:
Ever and anon the Lord dwelleth within thee.

Slok, 6; page 1426

8

sukh dukh jeh parsai nahi, lobh moh abhman

>Not cast down by sorrow
>Nor over-elate in joy;
>Aloof from the power
>Of pride, greed, and coveting:
>Such a man, saith Nānak,
>Is the image of God.
>
>*Slok*, 13; page 1326

9

bhai kahu ko det nāhi

>Who frighteneth none,
>Nor himself feareth any,
>Such a man, saith Nānak,
>Set him among the wise!
>
>*Slok*, 16; page 1427

10

sukh mai bahu sangī bhae dukh mai sang nā koe

Happiness and prosperity find many friends,
But adversity and sorrow have none,
Saith Nānak: Ponder on the Beloved, O my soul;
Even in the bitterness of death He is thy True Saviour!

Slok, 32; page 1427

11

jatan bahut mai kar rahio, mitio nā man ko mān

>Alas, all my efforts have come to nothing!
>I have not lessened my pride,
>I have not cast down my vanity:
>My mind is still the slave of evil impulses!
>Nānak prayeth: O Lord, save, save!
>
>*Slok*, 34; page 1428

12

ek bhagat bhagvān jah pranī

That man in whom there never kindles
One spark of the love of God,
Know, Nānak, that his earthly vesture
Is no better than that of a swine or dog!

Slok, 44; page 1428

13

nam rehio sādhu rehio, rehio gur gobind

The Word of God shall be everlasting;
The saints of God shall endure eternally;
So shall the Guru's glory be for ever secure.
In this world, saith Nānak,
Those that have endeared themselves to the Word,
Truly, they are few and far between!

Slok, 56; page 1429

HYMNS OF THE 'PRE-NĀNAK SAINTS'

I. KABIR
(1380-1460)

ॐ

Kabir, a weaver by profession, was born at Benaras of Mohammedan parents. Since a low-born Muslim like him could not meet an orthodox Brahmin saint like Ramanand, he hid himself on the steps of Ganges river, where Ramanand was accustomed to bathe. When he accidentally trod upon Kabir's body, Ramanand was deeply impressed by his humility and accepted him as his disciple. Kabir broke away from the orthodox formalism of his own Master and showed a frank dislike for institutional religion. Five hundred and forty-one hymns of Kabir are incorporated in the Adi Granth.

1

nagan phirat jau pāyai jog

If by going about naked
One could obtain unity
With the Supreme Lord,
All the beasts of the wild wood
Would be among the saved.

What does it matter
Whether a man goes naked
Or wraps himself in skins,
So long as the spirit of God
Is not realized within him?

If merely by shaving one's head
One could become perfect,
When the sheep are shorn
Why should they not be saved?

If one could obtain salvation
Merely by remaining continent,
Eunuchs should automatically
Reach the supreme state!

Saith Kabir: Listen, my brothers.
None has obtained salvation
But through God's Holy Name!

Rag Gauri, page 324

2

garbvās mai 'ul nahī jātī

In the womb of his mother
No man knoweth his caste;
All men are born
From God's One Spirit.

Tell me, O Pandit,
When became you a Brahmin?[1]
Waste not all your life
Insisting that you are so.

You say you are a Brahmin
Born of a Brahmin woman?
Should you not have come into the world
By another way?

What makes you a Brahmin
And I merely a Sudra?
If blood runs in my veins,
Does milk flow in yours?

Saith Kabir: Only he
In my estimation
Is a true Brahmin
Who meditateth on God!

Rag Gauri, page 324

3

hirdai kapat mukh gyāni

In your heart is deception
Though you talk of Divine Wisdom.
What does it avail you, hypocrite,
To be always churning water?

What spiritual gain do you get from
Scrupulously washing your body
When your heart remains unclean?

A gourd may be taken to bathe
In each of the sixty-eight
Holy places of pilgrimage,
But even so it will never
Lose its bitter taste!

[1] Brahmins claim to be born straight from the mouth of Brahma

Saith Kabir, in deep meditation:
Help me, O Lord, to cross
The troubled seas of the world!

Rag Sorath, page 656

4

bhūkhai bhagat nā kījai

I cannot concentrate
On my devotions to Thee
When I am faint with hunger.
Take back, Lord, this rosary.
I yearn only for the dust
Upon the feet of Thy Saints,
Since only to Thee, and to no man,
Am I under obligation.

O Lord, what shall I do
That I may be reconciled to Thee?
If Thou givest me not
What my hunger craves for,
I shall have to beg it of Thee!

I beg for two seers of flour,
A quarter of a seer of clarified butter and salt,
And half a seer of lentils
To feed me just twice a day!

I beg for a cot
With four short legs to it,
A pillow, a mattress,
A quilt to cover me.
And then Thy servant will be able
To concentrate on his prayers.

I have never been really greedy.
The Divine Name is the only thing I really hanker for.
Kabir says: My inner self is happy,
And when this is so, then I recognize God!

Sorath, page 656

5

aval allāh nūr upāyā kudrat ke sabh bande

The Lord first created Light:
From the Lord's play all living creatures came,
And from the Divine Light the whole creation sprang.
Why then should we divide human creatures
Into the high and the low.

Brother, be not in error:
Out of the Creator the creation comes:
Everywhere in the creation the Creator is:
The Lord's Spirit is all-pervading!

The Lord, the Maker, hath moulded one mass of clay
Into vessels of diverse shapes.
Free from taint are all the vessels of clay
Since free from taint is the Divine Potter.

The True One pervadeth all things.
All things come to pass as the Lord ordaineth.
He who hath understood the Divine Will
Recognizeth only the One Reality
And he alone is what man ought to be.

The Lord, being Unknowable, cannot be comprehended,
But the Guru hath given me
A sweet joy of His Presence.
Kabir saith: My doubts have departed from me.
In all things I have recognized the Taintless One.

Prabhati, page 1349

6

kabīr merī jāt ko sabh ko hasne hār

Kabir, all men mock at me for my low caste:
I am as a sacrifice unto this caste
In which I repeat my Maker's Name!

Slok, 2; page 1364

215

7

kabīr aisā ek ādh

Kabir: there are very few men indeed
Who are as dead to the world while still alive in it!
And who fearlessly sing the glory of God:
Wheresoever they look, there God is!

Slok, 5, page 1364

8

kabīr sabh te ham bure

Kabir: I am the worst of men:
Except myself, everyone is good!
He who humbly thinketh this of himself
Know him, O Kabir, to be my friend.

Slok, 7, page 1364

9

kabīr santan ki jhugiā bhalī

Kabir: The cottage of the saint is comfortable.
The village owned by the wicked man is a furnace.
May fire play upon these lofty mansions
Where the Name of the Holy Lord is not heard!

Slok, 15, page 1365

10

kabīr pāpī bhagat na bhāvīyai

Kabir: A sinner is averse to the love of God:
The worship of God has no charms for him.
He is like a fly that avoids sandalwood
And searcheth out foul odours.

Slok, 68, page 1368

11

kabīr jahān gyān teh dharm hai

Kabir, where there is divine knowledge there is righteousness:
Where there is falsehood, there is sin.
Where there is covetousness, there is Death;
Where there is forgiveness, there the Lord is.

Slok, 155, page 1372

12

kabīr māyā tajī to kyā bhayā

Kabir, what good does it do you to have given up
Love of the world, if you have not given up pride?
Seers and sages have perished by pride:
Their pride utterly consumed them!

Slok, 156, page 1372

13

kabīr mullāh munāre kyā cadhe

Kâbir, why, O Mullah, climbest thou up to thy minaret?
Thinkest thou that the Lord is hard of hearing?
Seek in thy heart for Him for whose sake
Thou so loudly callest to prayer!

Slok, 184, page 1374

14

nīoai loin kar rahoṅ le sūjun ghul māhi

Kabir, I cast down mine eyes modestly
And I take my Beloved into my heart:
I enjoy every delight with my Beloved,
But I keep my delight secret from all men!

Slok, 234, page 1374

217

15

āṭh jām causaṭh gharī tua nirkhat raho jīo

For the eight watches, the sixty-four *gharīs* of the day,
My soul, O Lord, looketh ever towards Thee!
Why should I ever cast my eyes down modestly
Since I behold the Beloved in all things?

Slok, 235, page 1374

II. SHEIKH FARID
(1173-1265)

Sheikh Farid was born at Khotwal near Multan. His father Sheikh Jalaludin was the nephew of the King of Ghazni. His mother Mariam provided the chief religious influence on him which directed his mind to the pursuit of truth.

At the age of sixteen he went to Mecca, and a few years later he adopted Qutab Din of Delhi as his Master (Pir) from whom he learnt the discipline and doctrine of the Sufis. On his Master's death he inherited his patched mantle.

He spent most of his time at Jodhan, later known as Pak Pattan and died at the age of 92, leaving 134 hymns in Punjabi which were procured by Guru Nānak from Sheikh *Ibrahim*, the twelfth successor of Farid and later preserved in the Adi Granth.

1

tap tap loh loh hath maroroṅ

I burn and writhe in agony,
I wring my hands in despair,
I am crazed with a longing for the Lord.
You forsook and You had a cause,
For I was in error, not Thou, O Lord.
For such a Sire as Thee little did I care,
When my youth faded, I fell into despair.
Black Koel what burnt thee so black?
The fire of separation from the Lord.
Without the Lord how can one cheer?
Through His mercy does one meet Him.
The world is a deep and dark pit of sorrow,
I a lonesome maid, without friend and companion.
In holy company I came by His grace.
I see God anew both as friend and mate.
Too arduous is the path I have taken,
Sharper than the double-edged sword,
Much sharper and keener,
That path you must take.
O Sheikh Farid, awake
Arise and think of Him.

Rag Suhi, page 794

2

farīdā je tū akal latīf

Farid, if thou hast discretion,
Note not with a blackmark
The ill deeds of thy neighbour,
Look first in thy own heart.

Slok, 6, page 1378

3

farīdā jo taiṅ māran mukīaṅ

Farid, should any man smite thee,
Return not blow for blow,
Nay, kiss his feet that smiteth thee,
And go peacefully homeward.

Slok, 7, page 1378

4

farīdā jā lab tā neh kīā

Farid, where there is greed,
How can there be true love?
How long will a leaking roof
Shelter Thee from rain?

Slok, 18, page 1378

5

farīdā jangal jangal kīā bhavaiṅ

Farid, why wandreth thou,
From jungle to jungle,
Breaking the thorny branches,
In search of thy Lord?
In thy heart and not in the jungle
Thy Lord doth reside.

Slok, 19, page 1378

6

farīdā galīai cikaḍ dūr ghar

Farid, the rain hath churned the road,
Distant is the Beloved's house
If thou goest to Him, thou wettest thy garments,
If thou remainest at home
Thou breakest the ties of love.

Slok, 24, page 1379

7

bhījo sijo kamblī alloh varsau meh

Let the rains come down in torrents, Lord,
And pelt and drench my garments,
Yet I go to meet the Beloved Friend
Lest I break the ties of love.

Slok, 25, page 1379

8

farīdā bure dā bhalā kar

Farid, return good for evil,
Let not the sun go down upon thy wrath,
Thy body shall then be free from sorrowing,
All things thou most desirest thou shalt have.

Slok, 78, page 1382

9

farīdā mai jāniā dukh mujh ko

Farid, I thought I alone had sorrow,
Sorrow is spread over the whole world.
From my roof-top I saw
Every home engulfed in sorrow's flames.

Slok, 81, page 1382

III. NAMDEV
(1269-1344)

Namdev was born at Narsi Bamni in Maharashtra. A tailor by profession, he turned to the religious life when still quite young. He had close associations with the famous ascetic scholar Gyan Dev, and the poetess Janabai. He was imprisoned by Sultan Mohammed bin Tughlak, but he refused to give up his faith. He was set free when the Sultan became convinced of his spiritual greatness. Namdev spent about ten years in the Punjab. He died at Pandharpur. There are 60 hymns by Namdev in the Adi Granth, a number of which are autobiographical.

I

ānīle kumbh, bhrāīle ūdak

If I should bring a pitcher,
Fill it with water
And go to bathe the idol,
Half of the world's living creatures
Live in the water;
God pervades them all,
Why need I bathe
His image with water?

Wherever I go,
God is contained there,
In supreme bliss
He ever sporteth.

If I should bring flowers
And make of them garlands
To honour the idol,
The bee has sucked the flowers,
God is in the bee;
Why should I weave
For His image a garland?

If I should bring milk
And cook rice in it
To feed the idol,
The calf has already
Made the milk impure
By tasting of it,
God is in the calf,
Why to His image
Need I offer milk?

God is with us here,
God is beyond us there,
In no place is God not,
Nama bows to the Omnipresent
Who filleth the whole earth.

Rag Asa, page 485

2

sāmp kuṅc chodai bikh nāhī chodai

The snake sloughs its old skin
But never gets rid of its poison.
Thou, since thy heart is not pure,
Why seemest thou to meditate,
Repeating the Holy Name?
The crane standing on one leg,
Still in the water,
Seemeth likewise to meditate.
She watcheth for fish!

The man who like a lion
Liveth by plunder,
Let gangs of robbers
Set him up for their saint!

Nama's Lord
Hath solved this riddle.
If thou would'st be pure,
O thou hypocrite one,
Drink the nectar of God's Name!

Rag Asa, page 485

3

mārwāḍ jesaī nīr bāhlā

As water is precious
To the traveller in Marwar,
As the hungry camel
Yearns for the creeper,
As the wild deer at night
Hearken enrapt
To the hunter's bell,
So God is the object
Of the yearning of my soul!

Thy Name is beauty,
Thy Form is beauty,
Thy Hues are beauty,
O my living Lord!

As the dry earth yearneth
In thirst for the raindrops,
As the honey-bee yearneth
For the scent of the flowers,
As the kokil loves the mango-tree,
So I long for the God.

As the sheldrake
Longs for sunrise,
As the swan yearneth
For Mansarowar Lake,
As the wife pines
For her husband,
So God is the object
Of the yearning of my soul!

As the babe yearneth
For his mother's breast-milk,
As the chatrik who drinketh
Only the raindrops
Yearneth for the rain,
As the stranded fish
Yearneth after water,
So God is the object
Of the yearning of my soul!

All seekers, sages, teachers
Yearn, O Lord, after Thee.
How few of them have seen Thee!
As Thy Name is yearned after
By Thy whole vast creation,
So for Nama God is the object
Of the yearning of his soul!

Rag Dhanasari, page 693

4

mai andhle kī tek terā nām khundkārā

To me who am like a blind man,
Thy Name, O Lord, is my staff.
Poor I am: most poor and wretched.
Thy Divine Name is as my sustenance.

O bountiful and merciful Lord, Thou art wealthy:
Omnipresent Lord, I humbly wait on Thy goodness!

Thou art the river of life for me.
Thou art the Great Giver, fabulous Thy wealth.
It is Thou who givest, Thou who takest.
There is none else besides Thee.

Thou art wisdom and Thou art Foresight:
How can I comprehend Thee?
O Nama's Lord, O dear God,
Thou art He who Forgivest!

Rag Tilang, page 727

5

ānīle kāgad kātīle gūdī

A boy gets paper, makes a kite,
He flies it high in the air,
And though he is still talking
In a lively way with his playmates,
He keeps his mind on the string!

Pierced with God's Name, I keep my mind on it
As a goldsmith does on his craft!

Young girls bring pitchers
To fill them at the city well,
And talk and laugh as they carry them
But keep their minds on the pitchers.

The cows go out of the many gates of the city,
They graze five miles away from their barns,
But they keep their minds on their calves:

Saith Namdev: Listen, O Trilochan!
While the child is asleep in its cradle
Inside and outside the house
His mother is very busy,
But she keeps her mind on her child.

Rag Ramkali, page 972

IV. RAVIDAS
(Fifteenth Century)

Ravidas was a cobbler by profession and a disciple of Ramanand. He resembled in every respect St. Boehme, the cobbler mystic of the West. Members of the highest caste became his disciples, prominent among whom was Princess Jhali of Chitore. There are forty-one hymns by Ravidas in the Adi Granth, written in the vernacular Hindi of Uttar Pradesh.

1

tohī mohī, mohī tohī antar kaisā

Between Thee and me, between me and Thee,
How can there be likeness or difference?
Likeness or difference as between gold
And a bracelet made of it, as between water
And the waves that move on its surface!
Were I not a sinner, O Eternal Lord,
How couldst Thou have the title of Redeemer of Sinners?
Thou, O Lord, art the Searcher of hearts.
Through God, the Master, we know the saints, His Servants:
Through the servants of God, we know God.
Grant me O Lord that my body may be Thy shrine.
Few, O Ravidas, see God in everything.

Siri Rag, page 93

2

begampurā ṣehar ko nāu

There is a place called City-of-no-Sorrows.
There is no grieving, no man suffers there.
There are no tax-gatherers. No one levies tribute.
There is no worrying, or sin, or fear, or death.
My friends, I have found myself a wonderful hometown
Where everything is good, everyone is happy!
There the sovereignty of the Lord is permanent
There all are equal, none second or third.
It is a populous and famous city.
The citizens are wealthy, and they move
As freely through the city as they please:
No high official of the palace impedes them.
My friends, says Ravidas, the emancipated cobbler,
Become my fellow citizens in this realm!

Gauri, page 345

3

kahaṅ bheo jau tan bheo chin chin

What would it matter that they rent my body?
Thy slave feareth only, Lord, that Thy Love may depart!
Thy feet are the lotus, and my soul flitteth
Like the honey-bees sucking their nectar,
   I have found my treasure!
Gains, losses, worldly desires and wealth
Shut us from God; Thy slave hath not become lost in them!
Thy slave is bound to Thee by the rope of Thy Love!
O Ravidas, how can it benefit thee
To seek to break free from His rope?

Rag Asa, page 486

4

jab ham hote tab tum nahī, ab tuhī mai nāhī

When I think of myself
Thou art not there.
Now it is Thou alone
And my ego is swept away.
As billows rise and fall
When a storm sweeps across the water,
As waves rise and relapse into the ocean
I will mingle with Thee.
How can I say what Thou art
When that which I believe is not worthy of belief.
It is as a King asleep on the royal couch
Dreams he is a beggar and grieves,
Or as a rope mistaken for Serpent causeth pain,
Such are the delusions and fears;
Why should I grieve,
Why be panic-stricken?
As a man who seeth several bracelets
Forgets they are made of a single substance, gold,
So I have been in error but am no more,
Behind all the various manifestations there is one God;
In the motions of every heart it is God that throbs.

Ravidas, He is nearer to us than our hands and feet!
As the Lord willeth, so all things come to pass!

Rag Sorath, page 657

5

nāgar janā merī jāt bikhyāt camāran

O people of the city everyone knows
I am a cobbler by trade and tanner by caste,
One of the low caste, and yet within my heart
I meditate upon God. If wine, which you think impure, is made
Of the holy water of the Ganges, you holy men
Will not drink it, but if that wine,
Or any other liquid you think impure,
Is poured in the Ganges, the river remains holy.
They make toddy from palms so the palm's leaves are impure
Yet if Holy Scriptures are written on paper made from palm-
  leaves
Men worship that paper, and bow before it.

Of low caste, by trade I am a cutter of leather:
In Benaras I carried dead cattle to the outskirts.
Yet noble Brahmins now bow low before me;
Since the slave, Ravidas, takes his shelter in Thy Name.

Rag Malar, 1293

V. RAMANAND
(1340–1430)

ੴ

Ramanand was born at Melukote near Madras and was the disciple of Raghvananda, the third in the spiritual descent from Ramanuja. Though he strictly practised most of Ramanuja's ethical principles he was more inclined towards his Bhakti-Cult than towards his Vedanta theology. He came to North India quite early in life and settled at Benaras. He tried to reconcile the personal mysticism of Islam with the Vaishnav theology of the Hindus, as a result of which the most prominent Hindu, Muslim and Pariah Saints of his time were his disciples. There is only one hymn by Ramanand in the *Guru Granth*.

kat jāīai re ghar lāgo rang

Whither need I go to seek holiness?
I am happy here within myself at home.
My heart is no longer a pilgrim:
It has become tied down to itself.

Restlessly one day I did want to go:
I prepared sandal-wood paste,
Distilled aloe wood, and many perfumes:
I set out towards a temple to worship:
Then my Guru showed me God in my own heart.

Whatever holy place I seek as a pilgrim
All I find is worship of water or stones,
But Thou, Lord, equally pervadest all things!
I have studied all the Vedas and the Puranas:
There or elsewhere thou mayest seek God
If God is not here in thy heart!

O gracious Guru, I am beholden unto thee
Who hast cut away my doubts and my vacillations!
Ramanand's Lord is the all-pervasive God:
The Guru's word removeth countless delusions.

Rag Basant, page 1195

VI. PARMĀNAND
(Fifteenth Century)

Parmānand was a Brahmin Vaishnavite disciple of Ramanand who lived at Barei near Sholepur. Though he is the author of innumerable poems, only one of his poems has been preserved in the *Adi Guru Granth*.

taiṅ nar kyā purān sun kīnā

Mortal man, what has been thy profit
From hearing the Puranas?
Thou hast not acquired a single-minded
Spirit of devotion to thy Lord!
Thou hast not given alms to the wretched.
Thou hast not put away thy lust.
Thou hast not put away thine anger.
Greed of gain has not left thee:
Thy lips are not clean of slander.
Thy outward shows of worship
Have all been utterly in vain.

Still thou robbest men on the roads
And breakest into men's houses to steal,
That thus, O criminal, thou mayest fill thy belly.
Fool, thou hast done such folly
As after death will earn thee an evil name!
From cruel violence thou hast not freed thy mind:
Thou hast not cherished mercy for living creatures.
Parmānand saith: In the company of the blest
Thou hast not joined in their holy speech!

Rag Sarang, page 1253

VII. SADHANĀ
(Late Thirteenth Century)

Sadhanā was a butcher of Sehwan in Sindh who made it a point to weigh the meat he sold with an idol, thereby belittling idol worship. Hated and condemned by the Brahmins and put to shame by a woman, he came to the Punjab where in all probability he met Namdev. He is said to have died the death of a martyr as he was bricked alive during the rule of the Sultans. His tomb is in Sirhind.

ਠਠ

nripkanyā ke kārnai

For the love of a King's daughter[1]
A man distinguished himself as Vishnu,
For the love of her and for his own ambitions:
Yet, Lord, Thou didst protect him from his shame!

[1] This refers to a well-known legendary story of a beautiful princess who was a great devotee of Lord Vishnu. She adored him so sincerely that she vowed she would marry no one but Vishnu. A young goldsmith fell in love with the princess and was determined to marry her. His ingenuity not only permitted him to build a helicopter-like swan such as Vishnu is accredited with having but he also made himself look like Lord Vishnu. Then on an auspicious day he landed on the palace roof near where the princess was standing. She rushed to worship at the impostor's feet and happily married him. The King was also extremely glad to have Vishnu as a son-in-law.

Since God Himself lived in the palace, routine matters were often neglected and affairs of state left to divine providence. Under these conditions the land was soon invaded by a neighbouring ruler. Although the King's armies were weak, he didn't worry because Vishnu would see that no disaster came to the Kingdom.

However, the invaders swept the weakened army aside and were soon at the wall of the capital city. Both the King and the Princess fell at Vishnu's feet and begged him to save the city but nothing happened and soon the enemy had taken the capital and was knocking at the palace door. At last the princess's tears flowed as freely as her pleas and the imposter could stand it no longer. He locked himself in the palace shrine and pleaded with Lord Vishnu to hear his anguished cries. He confessed his treachery and offered to accept his punishment. But he begged Lord Vishnu to save the country, pointing out the fact that if Lord Vishnu did not act and since the great Lord had been associated with the impostor's treachery, Vishnu would forever be associated with impotence. The impostor pleaded not for himself but for Lord Vishnu's reputation.

Vishnu, hearing the earnest and sincere prayers of a repentant soul, came to the city's rescue and it was miraculously saved.

Of what avail are Thy Powers,
O Lord of all the world,
If my sins cannot, like his, be forgiven?
What does it profit me
To seek for the Lion's help,
If the Lion still letteth the jackal devour me?

The chatrik, that bird
That can drink only raindrops,
Thirsteth in agony
For a single drop of water.
If when the bird dieth
He is given an ocean,
What can that avail him?

Now that my life is foundering
And will not last much longer,
How can I still be patient?
Will it help if a boat arrives
When I am already drowned?

I am nothing in myself;
I have nothing to offer;
There is nothing that by right
I can claim from Thee!
At this moment of desperation,
Sadhnā, Thy servant, prayeth:
Protect me, Lord, from shame!

Rag Bilawal, page 858

VIII. PĪPĀ
(1408-1468)

Pīpā was the ruler of Gagaraungarh State. Once he came to meet Ramanand with great pomp and show but the Saint refused to meet him. He then bestowed all his possessions on the poor and approached him with utter humility. He became a very devoted disciple and a friend of Kabir and Ravidas. There is only one hymn by Pipa in the Adi Granth.

kāyo devā kāyo deval kāyo jangam jātī
In the body, God is present.
The body is His temple.
In the body is the place of pilgrimage
Of which I am the pilgrim,
In the body is the incense and candles,
In the body is the holy offering,
In the body the oblation.

After searching in many regions
It is only in the body
I have found the nine treasures.
For me there is no going away,
For me there is no coming back,
Since I have appealed to God.

He who pervades the universe
Also dwells in the body:
Who seeks shall find him there.
Saith Pīpā: God is the Primal Being.
The True Guru shall reveal Him.

Rag Dhanasari, page 695

IX. SAIN
(1390–1440)

Sain was a court barber to the Prince of Rewa. After meeting Ramanand he gave himself more and more to contemplation and writing songs, so much so that he even started neglecting his court duty. The Prince was, however, very much impressed by his newly acquired spirituality and wisdom and accepted him as his Teacher and Guide. The court barber became the Court Guru.

※

dhūp dīp ghrit sāj ārtī

He who is worshipped with offerings
Of incense, lamps, and clarified butter,
To Him I am a sacrifice!

Hail, unto the Lord, all Hail!
Hail ever to the all-pervading Lord!

The choicest lamp and the purest wick
Art Thou alone, O Lord of Splendours!

It is Thy saints who know divine bliss,[1]
They speak of Thee as the all-pervading Primal Joy.
O God, whose beauty fascinateth me,
Waft me safely over the sea of terror.
Sain saith: Worship the Supreme Joy!

Rag Dhanasari, page 695

---

[1] *Rama bhagat ramanand janai:* Also explained by some as 'His befitting worship is known to Ramanand'. Ramanand was the Guru of Sain, the barber saint. Ramanand when not taken as a noun becomes 'rama' plus 'anand', or in English 'divine bliss'.

X. BHIKHAN
(1480–1573)

Sheikh Bhikhan was a Muslim Sufi saint who was learned in Islamic theology and had committed the whole of the Koran to memory. He appears to have been strongly influenced by Kabir and the Sufi disciples of Sheikh Farid. There are only two hymns by Bhikhan in the *Adi Guru Granth*.

naino nīr bahai tan khīnā

Tears trickle down from my eyes.
My body has become enfeebled.
My hair is as white as milk.
My throat is choked, when I try to speak
I falter, Lord, what shall I do?

O Sovereign Lord, Protector of the world,
Be Thou my healer, and save Thy saints!
My heart is in extreme anguish:
My head aches; my body is in a fever.
I am in such a state of pain
No human medicine can cure me.

The Name of God, that is pure nectar,
Is in the end the best of all medicines.
Saith Bhikhan: Through the grace of the Guru alone
Shall we reach the harbour of our salvation!

Sorath, page 659

XI. JAIDEV
(Twelfth Century)

Jaidev, the well-known author of Gita-Govinda was a native of Kinduviloa or Kandoli in Burdwan, and the most distinguished poet in the court of Lakshman Sen. The beauty and tender love of his wife appears to have inspired him with the gripping and lyric drama and mystical allegory of Gita Govinda. There are only two hymns by Jaidev in the *Adi Guru Granth*. The language of these hymns is a mixture of Prakrit and apbhraṅsh. Lassen and Pischal believe that even the original Gita-Govinda was in Prakrit and Apabhraṅsh, and it was given Sanskrit form much later.

parmād purkh manopamaṅ sat ādi bhavrataṅ

Primal Being, sublimely beautiful,
Primal Truth, all pervading,
Supremely wonderful, transcending nature:
Why then not contemplate Him, the Redeemer.
Devote thy mind only to the Holy Name
Which is ambrosia and the essence of life.
For those who remember the Lord
There is no fear of birth, of old age, and of death.

If thou desirest to defeat the angel of death
And all his ministers,
Praise and bless Thy Lord,
And do virtuous deeds.
The bliss of the Lord is unchanging
Now, and in the past, and in the future.

Man, if thou seekest to do virtuous deeds
Renounce thy greed, renounce thy coveting
Of thy neighbour's wife, all sins, all sinful desires.
And make the Lord thy refuge!

In heart and in words and in deeds
Devote thyself solely to thy Beloved Lord.
Without such devotion, what profit is there
In yoga, temple rituals, alms, and austerities?

O man, repeat the Sweet Name of the Beloved
Who is the bestower of all power upon men!
Jaidev openly seeketh his refuge in Thee:
Who art now, hast been, and Who pervadest all!

Gujri, 526

XII. BENI
(Fourteenth Century)

Beni was in all probability a contemporary of Namdev. A scholar and a poet with no livelihood, he told his wife that he was employed by the Raja for the interpretation of scriptures but every day he went to the forest for quiet meditation. But as he brought no money home, she became impatient. It is said that by strange circumstances Beni was given an honourable post and led a happy, saintly life.

tan candan mastak pāti

The body thou smearest with sandal paste,
And on the forehead thou stickest basil leaves,
But in thy heart thou hidest a murderer's knife.
Thou lookest on folk like a thug, deceptively;
Like a crane watching for fish, thou watchest thy neighbours.
Yet such a profound devotee thou seemest to be
Thy very breath seemeth suspended in meditation!

Thou bowest for a long time before the beautiful idol;
But thou hast an evil eye, and thy nights
Are given over to quarrelling.

Thou bathest thy body every day,
Keeping two dhotis, performing every ritual;
Thy speech is sweet as milk,
Thy heart like a drawn dagger;
It is thy way to cheat thy neighbours of their cash!

Worshipping stones,
And making circles of flour to honour Ganesh,
Thou keepest vigil all night
To take thy share in the *ras lila* service,
Thy feet dance, but thy heart planneth wickedness:
Sinful is such a dance, O sinful man!

On the deer skin thou sittest,
With a rosary of sacred basil,
Scrupulously clean are thy hands,
On thy forehead are religious marks,
But falsehood is in thy heart:
O wicked man, not in this way
Wilt thou earn the greetings
Of the Lord Krishna.

He who has not known the Supreme God
He is blind, and all his observances are vain,
Saith Beni, enlightened by the Guru, meditate on God!
Without the True Guru none find the way.

Rag Prabhati, page 1351

XIII. DHANNĀ
(Fifteenth Century)

Dhannā was a farmer born at Dhuan in the State of Tonk near Deoli. This little peasant boy had a very innocent soul. Seeing a Brahmin leading a very comfortable living by merely worshipping the idol he also sought the grace of God by worshipping the stone. For six days and nights he sat in meditation, and the God he sought in the stone revealed Himself within him. For further guidance in spiritual life he became the disciple of Ramanand. There are four hymns by Dhannā in the *Adi Guru Granth*, mostly against idol worship.

ॐ

bharamat phirat bahu janam bilāne

In error and illusion I have passed many lives;
My body, my mind, my worldly possessions are transient.
Held and defiled with the sins of greed and lust
I have forgotten God, the diamond.
To the crazed mind the fruits of sin are sweet:
It hath forgotten discrimination.
My passions, turning away from virtue, grow stronger:
Again I am weaving the cycles of birth and death.

I did not know the way of Him who dwelleth in the heart;
I burned with sin and fell into Death's noose.
I gathered the fruits of sin, and filled my heart with them.
There was no room left in it for the Supreme God.

Then the Guru caused the supreme treasure
Of knowledge of God to enter into my heart.
I centred my mind on the Lord in deep absorption,
It entered into my heart that He is One.
Embracing His love and service, I knew comfort:
I was satisfied, I was sated, I was set free.

He whose heart is filled with that Divine Light
Which also filleth creation,
He recognizeth the One
Who transcendeth all illusions.
Dhannā hath obtained God as his treasure:
And in the company of the Lord's saints
He hath become at one with the Lord.

Rag Asa, page 487

XIV. TRILOCHAN
(1267–1335)

Trilochan was a friend and contemporary of Namdev and both of them lived in close association with each other. Trilochan was initiated into religious life by Gyan Dev but was introduced to mystic life and experiences by Namdev. He had a quarrelsome wife and although he tried to give her all worldly comforts and the attention she demanded, he refused to pray for a son for her. There are four hymns of Trilochan in the *Adi Guru Granth*.

antar mal nirmal nahi kīnā

Thou who hast not cleansed the dirt from thy heart,
Why wearest thou the outer garb of a hermit?
And thou who in the unfolding lotus of thy heart
Hast not enclosed thy Lord,
Why hast thou adopted complete renunciation?

And thou, learned Brahmin, Jai Chand,
Thou hast gone astray in error and illusion;
For all thy learning, thou knowest not
God as the Primal Joy:

Thou, yogi, eating in every house
Hast fattened only thy body;
For gain thou wearest thy patched coat.
For gain thy beggar's ear-rings.
Thou hast rubbed thyself with the ashes
Of the dead from the cremation ground,
But since thou hast no Guru
Thou hast not found the One Reality!

All of ye, why these holy mutterings?
Why practise all these outward penances?
Ye might as well all churn water!
Remember the Lord in His Peace
Who hath made the millions of worlds!

Why, O holy beggar, carrying thy water-pot
Trudgest thou to the sixty-eight holy places?
Trilochan says: Listen, O foolish mortals!
What does it avail to thrash husks instead of corn?

Rag Gujri, page 525

8

HYMNS OF THE 'CONTEMPORARY SAINTS'

I. MARDANA
(1460–1530)

Mardana was a Muslim, a professional rebeck player of the village Talwandi, who played and sang folk songs only to beg his food from door to door. Guru Nānak asked him to give up begging and string his music to his divine song to which Mardana readily agreed. With his blunt manners and wit like that of Shakespeare's Touchstone, Mardana accompanied Guru Nānak on his long Missionary journeys, particularly his visit to the Muslim World of the Middle East. Mardana died at Kartarpur about nine years before Guru Nānak passed away. Besides the succeeding Sikh Gurus, Mardana is the only Sikh disciple who was permitted to use Guru Nānak's name in his hymns. Guru Angad addressed himself as Nānak the Second, while Mardana addresses himself as Mardana Nānak I. This abiding bond between Mardana and the Guru is expressed in all the three hymns of Mardana we have in the *Adi Guru Granth*.

kāyāṅ lāhan āp mad

In the vat of the body
Egoism is the wine,
Desire and low cravings
Are its companions.
The cup of ambition is
Abrim with falsehood.
And the god of death
Is the cup bearer;
By drinking this wine O Nānak,
One gathers multiple sins.

Make knowledge your yeast,
The praise of God the bread you eat
And the fear of God your meat.
This, O Nānak, is the true spiritual food.
Make divine Name your sustenance.

Var, Bihagra; page 553

II. SATTA AND BALWAND

Satta and Balwand were Muslim Bards who were also probably father and son. Being adept in Classical Music they were employed by Guru Angad to sing divine hymns. When young Guru Arjan became the Guru, they once demanded an exorbitant sum of money for the marriage of their daughter out of the public funds, which the Guru refused. They 'went on strike', thinking that the popularity of the Guru depended upon them. The Guru henceforth asked his disciples to learn music and never depend on the professional bards. Satta and Balwand soon repented. They have given a joint composition of eight hymns which tells us a good deal about Guru Angad and the reasons why Guru Nānak selected him as his successor in preference to his sons, and also explaining the unity of spirit in all the Gurus.

ॐ

lehne dī pherāīaī nānak dohī khatyai

Because of the devoted service of Lehna
Nānak proclaimed him as his successor.
The same divine light of Nānak shines in Him.
His ways of life are the same,
Only the body he has changed.

An umbrella of spiritual sovereignty,
Is held over his head,
As he occupies the throne of Guruship.
With unstinted devotion he served Guru Nānak,
And followed the arduous path
Leading to union with God.

Food was given free
From the Guru's inexhaustible store.
Out of the infinite gifts of the Lord,
He himself partakes much
And bestows freely on others.

The praises of God are sung,
And His grace like light descends from heaven;
A glimpse of you, O True King,
Is enough to wash the sins of thousands of births.
Truly has Guru Nānak made Angad his successor
How can we desist from proclaiming this truth;
Guru Nānak's sons did not obey him
They turned their backs to the True Guru.
Insincere were their hearts,
Defiant were their attitudes,
Loads of sins they carried on their heads.
Guru Nānak appointed him as the Guru,
Through him, Nānak himself reigns as the Guru;
He who has imparted the Guruship,
Has brought about all this;[1]
Lo, who has won and who has lost?

Ramkali Var Satta Balwand, page 966

---

[1] Succession of Guruship was open both to the sons as well as the disciples of the Guru. Guru Nanak's sons always showed vanity and pride of birth and position when put to test by the Guru while his disciple Lehna won the Guruship through humility, service and the spirit of self-sacrifice. Lehna was named Angad (meaning a part of his own self) by Guru Nanak, when he bequeathed on him the Guruship about six months before his death.

III. SUNDER
(1560–1610)

Sunder, the great-grandson of Guru Amardas was 14 years old at the time of the Guru's death. The last words of Guru Amar Das made a deep impression on him and he later on wrote a Sadd (lit. 'The Call'), an Elegy, giving the Sikh view of death, and pointing out that death is a moment of rejoicing for an enlightened soul when he is to meet the Beloved. This is the only composition of Sunder in the *Adi Guru Granth*.

ॐ

satgur bhāne apne beh parwār sadāyā

As Guru Amardas sat up
And of his own sweet will
He sent for his family and disciples:
Let no one weep for me
After I breathe my last:
That would not please me in the least.
A friend who desires his friend to be esteemed
Is pleased when his friend
Goes to the Lord to receive the robe of honour.
Reflect then my children and brothers
Is it good to weep and wail
When God adorns the Guru
With a robe of honour.

Guru Amardas while alive,
Appointed the successor to his spiritual throne;
He made all his disciples, relations, sons and brothers,
Bow at the feet of Ramdas.

Ramkali Sad, page 923

IV. SURDAS
(Sixteenth Century)

Surdas was Brahmin Saint whose scholarship and poetic talent won for him the Governorship of Sandila during the reign of Akbar. In his extraordinary zeal for charity he emptied the treasury of the State and absconded leaving a poem in the treasure chest. He was arrested and imprisoned but another poem addressed to Akbar soon secured him his freedom, He spent the rest of his life at Benaras. We have only two poems by Surdas in the *Guru Granth*.

ਠਃ

har ke sang basai har lok

Those whom God has chosen
Dwell ever in Him,
To Him they dedicate body and soul,
To Him they dedicate all possessions,
And while they exalt His Name
They enjoy divine rapture.

On beholding the Lord
A man is set free
From all sinful cravings
And all his desires are fulfilled.
One has no need of anything else,
Having gazed on His Beauty.

But they who forsake the Beauteous Lord
And set the desires of their hearts
On any other object,
Are like leeches sucking a leper!
O Surdas, God hath taken thy soul in His keeping
And hath blest it with His Kingdom!

Sarang, page 1253

V. KALSHĀR
(Sixteenth Century)

Kalshār was the leader of ten other Bard Poets of Uttar Pradesh, who speak about Guru Angad and the successive Gurus from personal knowledge. All these bards composed these poems during the time of Guru Arjan, but those who had some personal contacts with the previous Gurus speak about them also. All of them were good scholars of Sanskrit, Prakrit, Apabhrańsh, learned poets, and they were genuine seekers of truth who had wandered all over India for the light of God and had found peace at the feet of the Guru. Nothing is known about them except what the 122 poems contributed by them tell us.

༄༅

amyā driṣṭ ṣubh karai harai ag pāp

The nectar-laved glance of Guru Angad
Ennobles man. It destroys all sins and vice,
Lust, wrath, greed, and attachment are subdued
By its great power;
Abiding felicity fills the heart of the Guru;
He destroys the sorrows
And sufferings of the world.
The Guru is the treasure of all treasures;
He is the river that washes the dross of life.
So Bard Kal says:
Serve ye the Guru day and night
With tender loving.
In association with the Guru
His transmuting touch will destroy
The pangs of ceaseless births and deaths.

Swaiya Guru II; 2, 10, page 1392

VI. JĀLAP
(Sixteenth Century)

caran ta par skyath, caran gur amar pavalrya

Blessed are the feet,
Which lead one to Guru Amardas;
Blessed are the hands,
That touch the holy feet of the Guru;
Blessed is the tongue
Which sings the glory of Guru Amardas;
Blessed are the eyes,
Which have the opportunity to look at him;
Blessed are the ears which listen to his words;
Blessed is the heart,
In which is enshrined the Guru;
Guru Amardas truly is, the Divine Father of the world,
Blessed is the head, says Jālap,
Which bows daily before the Guru.

Swaiya Guru III, 10, page 1394

VII. BHIKHĀ
(Sixteenth Century)

rehio sant haun tol

In search of a true saint,
I vainly wandered about;
Recluses I encountered many,
Sweet-tongued no doubt were they;
For full one year in this search I wandered.
None of them gave me the solace of spiritual light.
I heard them talk a lot of high ideals
But their practice was most disappointing.
Discarding the Name of God,
They indulged in worldly ways,
O, what need I say of them?
By the Grace of God
I have found Guru Amardas.
By Thy will I shall ever abide, O Guru.

Swaiya Guru III, 2, page 1395

VIII. SALH

(Sixteenth Century)

pehar smādh snāh gyān

Wearing the armour of concentration.
Mounting the steed of knowledge,
With the bow of righteousness in hand,
And the arrows of devotion.
You, O Guru Amardas, thus fought the battle.
With the Eternal Lord within your heart,
With the lance of Guru's word in your firm grasp
You have cut to pieces the evils,
Of lust, anger, greed, ego and delusion.
O thou son of Tejbhan, monarch of an honourable lineage,
The blessings of Guru Nānak, King of Kings, is on Thee.
Salh proclaims the truth,
Guru Amardas fighting thus has defeated
Satanic forces in the battle.

Swaiya Guru III, 1, 21, page 1396

IX. BHAL

(Sixteenth Century)

ghan har būṅd basūa romāval

Countless are the raindrops from the clouds,
Countless the vegetation on the earth,
Countless are the flowers which bloom in spring.
Unfathomable the depth of the Ocean,
Countless the waves and ripples of the rivers,
Countless the rays of the sun and moon.
With Siva-like meditation.
And the divine knowledge of the True Guru,
One may know all these things; says poet Bhal,
But your virtues, O Guru, are beyond comprehension.
You alone are your own peer.

Swaiya Guru III, 1, 22, page 1396

X. NALH

(Sixteenth Century)

ੴ

jam guru hoe val gyan ar dyānan par

When the Guru is on one's side,
Riches do not add to his greatness.
When the Guru is on one's side,
Millions of arms cannot harm him.
When the Guru is on one's side,
The Divine word illuminates the soul,
Thy servant bard, supplicates thus!
He who meditates on the Name day and night,
He who contemplates the Name in the heart,
He is released from the bondage of birth and death.

Swaiya Guru IV, 3, 7, page 1399

XI. GYAND

(Sixteenth Century)

sansār agam sāgar tulāh

This in my heart have I realized
Unfathomable Ocean is the world;
The Lord's Name is the boat
Which I acquired from the Supreme Guru;
The cycle of birth and death has ceased for me.
Whosoever attains this realization
The highest spiritual state they attain,
They discard avarice, greed and attachment to worldly wealth.
The torments of lust and wrath are no more for them;
They attain the Vision of God.
All delusions disappear
In a flock they see the cause of all causes.
Serve ye the True Guru Ramdas the Saviour,
Inscrutable are his ways.
Swaiya Guru IV, 3, page 1402

XII. BAL

(Sixteenth Century)

jih satgur simrant

Contemplating the Guru
All darkness is dispelled.
Contemplating the Guru
The Name of God fills the heart day after day.
Contemplating the Guru
Desires now burning are assuaged.
Contemplating the Guru
Occult powers, nine treasures and prosperity is attained;
Says poet Bal: that Guru is Ramdas.
Meeting in the holy congregation.
Let all say: Hail, all hail to the Guru,
Contemplate, O mortals, the true Guru,
In whose association God is realized.

Swaiya Guru IV, 5, 54, page 1405

XIII. MATHURĀ

(Sixteenth Century)

jab lau nahī bhāg lilār udai

As long as providence did not favour me,
So long I wandered restlessly;
In the dreadful ocean of the dark age
My helpless soul was sinking,
Sorrow and remorse never left me.
Arjan has come as the Saviour of the world.
My search for the True Guru Arjan has ended.
He who contemplates the divine Guru Arjan
Never is a victim of the tribulations of rebirth.

Swaiya Guru V, 6, 8, page 1409

XIV. KĪRAT

(Sixteenth Century)

ੴ

ham avguṇ bhare ek gun nāhī

Sins abound in me,
No virtues have I;
Forsaking the nectar
I drink poison,
I lost in error and delusion am,
Deeply attached to wife and children;
I heard of a lofty way
In the company of the Guru.
Meeting him the fear of death
Has ceased to exist.
Bard Kīrat hath but one prayer,
Keep me under your protection, O Guru Ramdas.

Swaiya Guru IV, 4, 58, page 1406

XV. HARBANS

(Sixteenth Century)

ajai gaṅg jal atal

Like the holy, the ever-flowing waters of the sacred Ganges,
Flow the sermons of the Guru.
In it bathe the congregations of the Sikhs.
The scriptures are explained and recited,
As if Brahma himself chanted the Vedas,
Over the Guru's head waves the royal umbrella.
From his lips Divine Name as nectar rains;
In the company of Guru Nānak,
Angad became the Guru,
Then after him Amardas;
And now Guru Ramdas has gone to the Lord;
O Harbans, his glory fills the whole world.
Who says the Guru is dead?

Swaiya Guru, V, 1, 20, page 1409

PART TWO

SELECTIONS FROM THE 'DASM GRANTH'

THE HYMNS OF GURU GOBIND SINGH
(1660-1708)

Guru Gobind Singh was born at Patna (Bihar) and was brought to the Punjab at the age of five. He took over Guruship at the age of nine when his father was executed by the Mughal Emperor Aurangzeb. He spent his youth in study of Sanskrit and Persian and the Indian scriptures. He was a great patron of letters and was himself a prolific writer.

On the Indian New Year's Day of 1699 he started the militant order of the Khalsa and thereafter his life became one long series of battles in which he lost his four sons (two were killed fighting; the other two aged eight and ten were executed). Despite these reverses he remained defiant to the last and left behind a powerful fighting force which later occupied most of the Punjab.

Guru Gobind Singh compiled the final version of the *Adi Granth*. His own writings, which do not form a part of the Sacred book, were collected by his disciple Mani Singh thirty years after the Guru's death. The compilation, which has over 2,000 hymns, is known as the *Dasm Granth*—the *Granth* of the tenth Guru.

1

cakra cehan ar barn jāt ar pāt nahinjai

God hath no marks or symbols,
He is of no colour, of no caste,
He is not even of any lineage.
His form, hue, shape and garb
Cannot be described by anyone.
He is immovable, He is self existent;
He shines out in His own splendour;
There is no one who can measure His Might.
He is the King of Kings, the lordly Indra
Of countless Indras, the supreme Sovereign
Of the three worlds of gods, men, and demons;
Nay, even the meadows and the woodlands
Cry in praise of Him: 'Infinite, Infinite!'
O Lord, who can tell the count of Thy Names?
According to Thy deeds will I
Endeavour to relate Thy Names.

Jap, 1

2

nāṁ thām nā jāt jākar rūp raṅg nā rekh

He has no name, no dwelling-place, no caste;
He has no shape, or colour, or outer limits.
He is the Primal Being, Gracious and Benign,
Unborn, ever Perfect, and Eternal.
He is of no nation, and wears no distinguishing garb;
He has no outer likeness; He is free from desire.
To the east or to the west,
Look where you may,
He pervades and prevails
As Love and Affection.

Jap, 80

3

kahāṅ bheo doū locan mūṅd ke

What does it profit you
To close both eyes
And to sit like a crane
In false meditation:
For you who go about
Bathing in the seven seas
To show your holiness,
This world is lost,
And the next world also!
You have passed your lives vainly
In the company of sinners!
Hear me, ye people! Hear the Truth!
They that truly Love God
They alone shall meet Him.
Akal Ustat, 9, 29

4

koū bheo mundia sanyāsī

One man by shaving his head
Hopes to became a holy monk,
Another sets up as a Yogi
Or some other kind of ascetic.
Some call themselves Hindus:
Others call themselves Musulmans.
Among these there are the Shiahs,
There are the Sunis also,
And yet man is of one race in all the world;
God as Creator and God as Good,
God in His Bounty and God in His Mercy,
Is all one God. Even in our errors,
We should not separate God from God!
Worship the One God,
For all men the One Divine Teacher.
All men have the same form,
All men have the same soul.
Akal Ustat, 85, 15

5

dehrā masīt soī, pujā au namāz oî

He is in the temple as He is in the mosque:
He is in the Hindu worship as He is in the Muslim prayer;
Men are one though they appear different,
Gods and demons who guard the treasures
Of the god of riches, the musicians celestial
The Hindus and the Muslims are all one,
Have each the habits of a different environments,
But all men have the same eyes, the same body,
The same form compounded of the same four elements,
Earth, air, fire, and water.
Thus the Abhekh of the Hindus and the Allah of Muslims are one,
The Koran and the Purans praise the same Lord.
They are all of one form,
The One Lord made them all.

Akal Ustat, 86, 16

6

jaise ek āg te kanukā kot āg uthai

As out of a single fire
Millions of sparks arise;
Arise in separation
But come together again
When they fall back in the fire.
As from a heap of dust
Grains of dust swept up
Fill the air, and filling it
Fall in a heap of dust.
As out of a single stream
Countless waves rise up
And, being water, fall
Back in water again.
So from God's form emerge
Alive and inanimate things
And since they arise from Him
They shall fall in Him again.

Akal Ustat, 87

7

khag khaṅd bihaṅdan khal dal khaṅdan

Sword, that smiteth in a flash,
That scatters the armies of the wicked
In the great battlefield;
O thou symbol of the brave.
Thine arm is irresistible, thy brightness shineth forth
The blaze of the splendour dazzling like the sun.
Sword, thou art the protector of saints,
Thou art the scourge of the wicked;
Scatterer of sinners I take refuge in Thee.
Hail to the Creator, Ṣaviour and Sustainer,
Hail to Thee: Sword supreme.

Bachiter Natak, 1

8

mai apnā sut toh nivājā

Thus spake God unto me:
I have cherished thee as My son
And ordained thee to spread the Faith.
Go and extend true religion throughout the world
And divert the people from the evil paths.

I made obeisance with folded hands,
I bowed my head, and I spake thus meekly:
'Thy religion, O Lord, shall prevail in the world
When Thou vouchsafest Thine help in its prevailing!'

For this mission God sent me into the world,
And on the earth I was born as a mortal.
As He spoke to me, I must speak unto men:
Fearlessly I will declare His Truth,
But without enmity to any man.

Those who call me God
Shall fall into the depths of Hell.
Greet me as God's humble servant only:
Do not have any doubts that this is true.

I am the slave of the Supreme Lord.
I have come to behold the wonders of His Play here.
That message that God has entrusted me with
That I will deliver;
And will not remain silent, through fear of men.

Whatever the Lord spake unto me,
That I shall surely speak unto men;
I will pay no regard to anyone but God,
I will not adopt the habit of any creed
But will sow the seeds of the pure love of God.

I will not bow down to worship sticks and stones,
Nor be influenced by outward piety;
I shall meditate on the Word of the Lord
And attain to the Presence of God.

Bachiter Natak (Autobiography), Chapter 6, Verses 29, 30, 31, 32, 33, 34, 35.

9

re man aiso kar sanyāsā

O man, practise asceticism after the following manner:
Think no more of thy house in the city
Than as if it were a forest abode;
And remain always a hermit in thine heart!
Instead of matted hair, cultivate continence;
Wash thyself daily in unity of will with God;
Let thy daily religious duties be thy long growing nails!
Let divine wisdom be thy Guru and enlighten your soul
As with ashes, smear thy body with the love of God!
Eat little, sleep little; be compassionate and forgiving;
Be calm and contented;
Then will you pass beyond the Three States.
Hold not close in your heart
Lust, anger, greed, obstinate selfhood or love of worldly things.
Then shalt thou behold that which is real
And attain to the One Lord.

Hazare Sabad

10

mitar pyare nū hāl murīdāṅ dā kehnā

Go tell the Beloved Lord
The condition of His yearning disciples;
Without Thee, rich coverings are an agony to us,
And to live in the comforts of our households
Is like living with snakes! Our water pots
Have become like pikes on which men are impaled.
The cup we drink from has an edge like a dagger!
Beloved, Thy turning away from us
Is like what a beast endures from the slaughterer!
With the Beloved, a mattress of straw would please us;
Without Him, in rich houses, we are burned alive!'

Hazare Sabad

11

jo kich lekh likhio bidhnā soī pāyat misar jū sok nivāro

All the battles I have won, against tyranny
I have fought with the devoted backing of these people;
Through them only have I been able to bestow gifts,
Through their help I have escaped from harm;
The love and the generosity of these Sikhs
Have enriched my heart and my home.
Through their grace I have attained all learning;
Through their help, in battle, I have slain all my enemies.
I was born to serve them, through them I reached eminence.
What would I have been without their kind and ready help?
There are millions of insignificant people like me?

True service is the service of these people:
I am not inclined to serve others of higher castes;
Charity will bear fruit, in this and the next world,
If given to such worthy people as these.
All other sacrifices and charities are profitless.
From top to toe, whatever I call my own,
All I possess or carry, I dedicate to these people!

Hearing this the learned Brahmin was ablaze.
Malice boiled in him and anger
Burnt as briskly as straw burns in flame.
He could not bear the thought
That by such levelling of castes
The Brahmins might lose their livelihood.
The Pundit wept and wailed
At the plight of his neglected order.

Hazare Sabad

12

jāgat jot japai nis bāsar

Inspired by devotion
And awake to the Light,
Singing perpetually
The Name of the Lord,
Having no faith in any
Except the One Lord,
Absorbed in His splendour,
Absorbed in His Love,
Even amid error
Never believing
In fasts and tombs,
Temples and idols,
Or in anything but
Devotion to the One:
Caring not even for
Compassion or charity
If God's life
Be not in them;
Not for penances,
Not for bathings
In the holy places,
Not for the yogi's
Self-macerations:
Such a child of Light,
Such a paragon,
Such a complete man,

Fully enlightened
In heart and soul
To be of the Khalsa
Is worthily deemed!

Teti Sweyas, I

13

deh sivā bar moh ehai subh karman te kabhuṅ nā taroṅ

Grant me this boon
O God, from Thy Greatness,
May I never refrain
From righteous acts;
May I fight without fear
All foes in life's battle,
With confident courage
Claiming the victory!
May my highest ambition be
Singing Thy praises,
And may Thy Glory be
Grained in my mind!
When this mortal life
Reaches its limits,
May I die fighting
With limitless courage!

Epilogue to *Chandi Chariter*, I

14

dhan jio teh ko jag mai

Glory to noble souls
Who on their earthly way
Carry upon their lips
The Name of the Lord,
And ever contemplate
Deep within their hearts
The good fight's spirit.

Knowing that the body
Is a fleeting vesture
They make the Lord's Song,
They make the Lord's Name,
A boat to carry them
Over life's rough ocean.
They wear as a garment
That is as a fortress
Serene detachment;
Divine knowledge
Is the light of their minds;
Their cleaner's broom
In their wise hands
Is the broom of wisdom.
With it they sweep
All cowardice
And all falsehood.

Epilogue to *Krishna Avtar*

15

pāe gaha jab te tumra tab te kou āṅkh tare nāhī āṅio

Ever since, O Lord, I took refuge at Thy Feet
I have not worshipped any other God!
Ram and Rahim: the Purans and the Korān call Thee,
The Vedas, the Simiritis and also the Shastras
Have multifarious names for Thee who art One!
But, O Lord, I have faith in none besides Thee!
O glorious wielder of the Sword of Justice,
Through Thy Grace, I have written this epic of Rama!

dohrā

After leaving all other doors, Lord, I have come to Thy Door!
O make me Thine, Since once Thou didst call me Thine Own:
I, Gobind, who am but Thy humblest servant!

Ram Avtar; Epilogue, 863, 864

GLOSSARY

ACĀR   custom; practice; external observance of established rules and laws.
ĀDI   primal; first; the beginning; origin.
ĀDI GRANTH   Holy Book of Sikhs. It was compiled by Guru Arjan in A.D. 1604 and finally completed and edited by Guru Gobind Singh in A.D. 1705. Just before his death in 1708, he crowned the Holy Book as Guru, and the *Adi Granth* was thereafter to be known as *Guru Granth*. It is considered to be the mystic personality of the Gurus, the voice of the immortal living Teacher.
AGYĀN   ignorance; spiritual blindness.
AKĀL   immortal; beyond death.
ALLĀH   God.
AMRIT (AMYA)   the elixir of immortality; nectar; ambrosial drink.
ANĀND   Spiritual delight; bliss of the spirit. Name of a composition of Guru Amardas.
ANHAD SABAD   Unstruck music; music of the spheres; celestial symphony; divine music heard within the soul by the mystics.
ĀRTĪ   a form of worship in which lamps placed in a salver are waved before the object of worship.
ARTH   material interest; one of the four objects of life in Hindu philosophy, the other three being kama (interest) dharma (ethical being) and mokh (liberation).
ĀṢAK   a passionately devoted lover.
ĀTMĀ   the self; the spirit; the inner being; the soul.
AVDHUT (AUDHUT)   mendicant; hermit; yogi of Gorakh School.
AVTĀR   birth; descent of a deity; incarnation; rebirth.
AVIDYĀ   ignorance.
AYĪ PANTH   a sect of yogis.
BABĪHĀ   same as chatrik.
BAGLA   crane; heron; an aquatic bird symbolic of hypocrisy.
BHAGAT (BHAKT)   saint.
BIRHĀ   pain; agony; suffering.
BRAHM, BRAHMA   (1) Supreme Reality; God. (2) the first member of the Hindu triad, the Creator.
BRAHMAN   the first of the four castes of the Hindu social order.
BRAHMAND (VARBHAND)   (lit. infinite egg or orb) the Universe.
BRAHM-GYANI   one who has perfect knowledge and experience of God; God illumined soul, who has attained highest spiritual state.
BUDHĪ   intellect; faculty which reasons and understands.
CHAKOR   the red-legged bartavelle or Greek partridge said to subsist on moonbeams.

CHAKVĪ a ruddy sheldrake, the bird eagerly waits for sunrise all night as it cannot see her mate in the darkness. This has given rise to the legend that in the pairs of sheldrake are enshrined the souls of erring lovers.

CARN-KAMAL (lit. lotus feet) symbolically meaning the first spiritual experience of Divine light.

CHATRIK, or SARANG or BABIHA or PAPEEHA hawk-cuckoo, or the brain-fever bird, found mostly in hilly tracts where there is water. It is said to remain thirsty as long as it does not get the raindrops from the clouds. Its repeated cry for the raindrops is symbolically used in the hymns of the Gurus as a heart intensely yearning for the love of God.

CHE GHAR six systems of the Hindus; see khat darsan.

CIT mind-stuff, that which contains and retains all the individualized mind; heart.

DAN charity.

DARBAR royal court; the Presence of God.

DARGAH the presence of God.

DARSAN (1) vision; a glimpse of divine light.
(2) philosophy; system.

DASM GRANTH it is a collection of the religious and secular works of Guru Gobind Singh, collected and compiled by his disciples and martyr saint Bhai Mani Singh, twenty years after his death. Although a number of works were lost and some of the works in this collection like Akal Ustat and Gyan Prabodh are incomplete yet it is a monumental collection in itself.

DAYĀ˙ mercy, compassion.

DHARAM (lit. that which holds together) righteousness; the spirit of truth; moral law; religion; duty; justice; the inmost constitution of nothing which determines man's conduct and his sense of right or wrong.

DHARAM RAJ or YAMA, AZRAEL the King of justice; regent of death.

DHRUVA Dhruva was the son of Utanpada who had two wives. Like his step-brother he one day tried to take a seat in the lap of his father, but he was contemptuously treated by the King and his favourite wife. The poor child went sobbing to his mother, who told him in consolatory terms that fortune and favour were not attainable without spiritual efforts. At those words the lad left paternal roof and in a forest retreat performed rigorous austerities. The great sage Narad, author of Bhakti Sutra, became his spiritual preceptor.

DHYAN concentration, meditation.

DOSĪ sinner.

GAGAN sky; firmament.

GANIKĀ   prostitute; generally refers to a particular prostitute who gave up her sinful life under the influence of a Saint and became an enlightened woman.

GUNĀS   attributes; constituent elements; the three modes of psychic status:—
(1) tamo: stupidity, laziness, inertia.
(2) rajo: passion, restlessness, aggressive activity.
(3) sato: tranquillity, purity, and calmness.

GORAKH   a great prophet of the Yogis who flourished in the tenth century. He was a follower of Dattatreya and Machhinder and started a sect of his own called the Kanpatta Yogis. Many of his followers also took up the name of Gorakh.

GURBANI, GURVANI   (lit. the utterances of the Guru) the hymns of the *Ādi Granth*, the voice of the Teacher.

GURMAT   philosophy or faith of the Gurus.

GURMUKH   (1) saint; enlightened seer, inspired with the Guru-given light; (2) Guru (3) God.

GURDEV   Guru, the Lord, spiritual father.

GYAN ANJAN   collyrium or the salver of Divine knowledge.

GYAN KHAND   the realm of divine knowledge.

HAJ   to make a pilgrimage to Mecca.

HARI   an attributive name of God.

HARI-NAM   Divine Name.

HUKAM   (lit. command) in Sikh theology it means the Will of God.

IṢK   love; intensive devotion.

JUG (YUGĀ)   cycle or age—there are four ages:—
(1) Satya Yug: Age of truth. Duration: 1,728,000 years.
(2) Treta Yug: Age in which three parts belong to the truth and one to untruth: 1,296,000 years.
(3) Dvapar Yug: The age in which truth and untruth are equal: 864,000 years.
(4) Kali Yug: The age of ignorance and spiritual darkness. The present age is considered to be kaliyuga: 432,000 years. This Yuga began in February 3102 B.C.

KARM KĀND   conventional religious practices.

KARM KHAND   realm of grace; the fourth realm out of the five realms of spiritual ascent explained in Japji.

KAVĀO   utterance; primal creative utterance of God.

KHĀLAS, KHĀLSĀ   pure; noble; enlightened; saint.

KHAT DARSHAN   six systems of Brahmanical philosophy:—
(1) Nyaya (2) Vaishishika; (3) Saṅkhya; (4) Yoga; (5) Purva Mimamsa; (6) Vedanta.

KHĀNĪ   sources of earthly life, considered to be four; egg, womb, sweat and seed.

LAKH   one hundred thousand.
LĀNVĀN   marriage hymns.
LIV   deep concentration, contemplative absorption, spiritual attitude of mind; opposite of liv in this sense is *dhat* which means material attitude of mind.
LOBH   greed; avarice.
MANMAT   to follow one's own bigoted views.
MANMUKH   self-willed; irreligious; unspiritual; he who turns away from divine path; antonym, gurmukh.
MANT, MANTAR   (1) mystic word; divine name of God; (2) magical formula.
MAĪ   (1) mother; (2) maya.
MANĪAIN   (lit. believing) reflection; an experience of an intuitionally manifest faith and an unshakeable confidence in God.
MĀYĀ   world stuff; material wealth, the veil covering reality; appearance or phenomena.
MOH   attachment; craving desire.
MUKTI (MOKSA)   liberation, salvation.
NĀDAM   sound; the inner music.
NĀM   Divine Name; the Word; *logos*; the spirit of God.
NAMĀZ   Muslim prayer.
NĀRADĀ   an Indian sage known for his devotion to God and for his cunning. Supposed to be author of Bhakti Sutra.
ONKĀR   the primal being; the Eternal source of life.
PANC   (1) five; (2) elect; (3) the chosen ones.
PANC TAT   five elements; air, fire, water, earth and ether.
PANTH   the way; path of life, a community of common faith.
PĀP   sins.
PĀRAS   the philosopher's stone by the touch of which the eight metals like iron, copper, turn to gold; used figuratively in *Ādi Granth* for the Divine Name.
PHIRANGI   Europeans.
PHARĀSISI   French.
QAZI   judge, adept in Islamic law.
RĀG   an Indian musical motif or fundamental air, feminine form ragni, personified lyric divinities. The *Ādi Granth* has been classified according to the ragas in the following order:—
   Sirirag; Majh; Gauri; Asa; Gujri; Devgandhari; Bihagra; Vadhans; Sorath; Dhansari; Jaitsiri; Todi; Bairadi; Tilang; Suhi; Bilawal; Gond; Ramkali; Nat Narayan; Mali Gauda; Maru; Tukhari; Kedara; Bhairon; Basant; Sarang; Malar, Kanada; Kalyan; Prabhati; Jaijavanti.
RĀMDĀSPUR   the holy city of Amritsar which was founded by Guru Ramdas.
RĀJ-YOGĀ   a life of spiritual union lived in full worldly glory.

RIDHĪ occult powers.
SAHAJ mental and spiritual equipoise without the least intrusion of ego; unshaken natural and effortless serenity attained through spiritual perfection.
SAKTI cosmic energy; force; nature; manifest creation is said to be made of Siv and Sakti, or spirit and material energy.
SANYĀSĀ asceticism; fourth stage in the Hindu four-fold way of life.
SARAM, SRAM (1) shame; humility; modesty; (2) effort; labour; struggle.
SARAM KHAND (1) realm of modesty (2) realm of spiritual efforts.
SATSANG (SADHSANGAT) communion with holy men; association with truth congregation.
SIDH hermit; adept in spiritual powers; a sect of yogis of Gorakh School.
SIDDHIS occult powers.
SIDH-GHOST a composition of Guru Nanak; meaning a dialogue with the sidhas.
SIMRIN contemplation; sempiternal remembrance of the Divine Name.
SIMRITI traditional and man-made Hindu laws; moral code as distinguished from sruti or revealed laws.
SINGH lion.
SIVA (1) Name of the third god of Hindu Trinity; (2) eternal being; impersonal goodness; spiritual essence.
SUD, SUDRA parhia; low caste.
SŪNĪAI (lit. hearing or hearkening) primary state of receiving the inspiration from the Guru or what is otherwise called the implanting of the word of God in the soul; communion with the word or inspiration of the word.
SUNYA void; the state when creation ceases and nothing but God exists.
TURYA beyond three states of mind; the fourth state, transcendent or highest spiritual state.
VAIRAG distaste for the world and life, cessation of attraction to the objects of the mind's attachments.
VART fasting.
VED, VEDA (lit. that which makes known the hidden high truths) the four sacred scriptures of Hindus; a holy book or scripture of highest order; the word in this poetic sense is used in *Ādi Granth* also.
VIDYA knowledge; learning.
VIS poison.

VISNU   preserver aspect of the Hindu Trinity; that which permeates pervades, binds, and holds together all individual souls and all things.
VAH   wonderful.
VANJARA   trader.
YOGA (JOG)   union; occult practices; Sahaj Yoga, Integral Yoga, aiming at spiritual union without discarding worldly life.
YUGA   See jug.

INDEX

	PAGE		PAGE
A boy gets paper, makes a kite	227	As long as providence did not favour me	262
A cow is no use without milk	85	As out of a single fire	269
A mother loves to watch her son eat	142	As the winter's snow	113
A scholar who sins will not be spared	92	As the word of the Lord descendeth upon me	96
A true Brahmin is one who grasps Brahm	118	As water is precious	225
A true Kṣatriya of the warrior caste	118	At sunset the birds gather in the branches	196
A union of bodies is no union	121	Beauteous Vaisākh	107
Accept first to die	200	Because of the devoted service of Lehna	250
After leaving all other doors, Lord	275	Behold the birds of the air	81
After wandering and wandering, O Lord	171	Between Thee and me, between me and Thee	230
Air like the Guru's Word gives us the breath of life	51	Blessed are the feet	255
Alas, all my efforts have come to nothing	209	Blessed beautiful is the Hut	190
All men cry 'Lord, Lord'	132	Both the fool who confers authority	116
All men have access to the Guru	134	Brahmin propitiate the saligram (Stone-God)	114
All men talk of bliss, but true bliss	128	By hearkening to the Name	33, 34
All shyness and hesitation has died away	98	By merit alone of our deeds	185
All the battles I have won, against tyranny	272	By remembering the Lord we obtain wealth	156
Allah's depths are not to be sounded	198	By the first nuptial circling (Marriage Hymns)	150
Among all men that man is foremost	158	But Yoga is a system	100
As a fish cannot live out of water	188	Celestial Music is heard in the blessed house	127
As a salve for our eyes	173	Contemplating the Guru	261
As a thirsting man yearneth for water	153	Countless are the raindrops from the clouds	258
As an actor in a play appears in many guises	189	Countless are Thy Names, countless Thine abodes	38
As Guru Amardas sat up	252	Countless times a day	91
As He was in the beginning: the Truth	28	Dark wood after dark wood I have groped through	179
As in the realm of Knowledge wisdom shines	49	Deep in me there is longing to see Thee	143

	PAGE
Entertain in the heart the fear of the Lord	83
Eternal is the city of my God-like Guru	191
Even as a pillar upholdeth a temple-roof	169
Even while living	100
Ever and ever, remembering, remember Thy Lord	155
Ever, ever, ever repeat the Name of the Lord	170
Ever since, O Lord, I took refuge at Thy Feet	275
Every beggar today would be a King	123
Everything is within oneself, nothing outside oneself	179
Exalt the Name of the Lord	174
Farid, I thought I alone had sorrow	222
Farid, if thou hast discretion	220
Farid, return good for evil	222
Farid, should any man smite thee	221
Farid, the rain hath churned the road	221
Farid, where there is greed	221
Farid, why wandereth thou	221
Five prayers, five times a day	77
Fix thy thoughts upon that loving God	160
For the eight watches, the sixty-four gharis of the day	218
For the love of a King's daughter	235
For those, O Nānak, it is perpetual spring	121
From sin, He is the Redeemer	208
From within, from within	103
Give up the ways that turn thee from God	95
Glory to noble souls	274
Go tell the Beloved Lord	272
God has His seat everywhere	47
God hath no form, outline or colour	169

	PAGE
God hath no marks or symbols	267
God made the night and the day	48
Going forth a begging	45
Grant me this boon	274
Hail, all hail to the True Guru, the Perfect	153
Hail to the Founder Guru, to the Primal One (Sukhmanī)	155
Happiness and prosperity find many friends	209
He cannot be installed like an idol	31
He has no name, no dwelling place, no caste	267
He Himself is the Creator	122
He in whose heart this Song of Peace indwelleth	175
He is a true Vaishnav	166
He is in the temple as He is in the mosque	269
He that remembereth the Lord	156
He who deems himself a Sikh of the true Guru	143
He who dies in the Word	139
He who in his heart ever loveth God's ordinances	167
He who is true in heart and speech	162
He who is worshipped with offerings	238
He who knoweth the True Being	170
He who preserveth the Lord's name in his inmost heart	166
He who taketh refuge at the feet of the saints	168
Hearkening to the Name bestows	34
His chosen are His saints, and great are they	36
How can steel be chewed with waxen teeth?	102
However handsome, well-born, wise	184
Humility is our spiked mace	187

	PAGE		PAGE
I burn and writhe in agony	220	In the womb of his mother	212
I cannot concentrate	214	In this age of darkness	115
I crave from Thee, Lord, the gift of Thy Name	189	In this Holy Book: the Adi Granth	201
I have described the realm of dharma	49	In your heart is deception	213
I have found the falseness	206	Infinite is His Goodness and infinite its praise	41
I have lost my nights in sleep	84	Innumerable are they who sing the praises of the Lord	167
I have never properly sung the praise of the Lord	208	Inspired by devotion	273
I left my home to look for a Saint	101	Invincible is the army of the saints	202
I neither keep the Hindu fast nor the Muslim Ramadān	200	It is in no one's power to give livelihood to another	81
I supplicate thee, my friend, to listen to me	63	It is not they who burn themselves alive	135
I was a minstrel out of work	82	It is not through thought that He is to be comprehended	29
I will be as the slave of him	148	It is the month of Chet	106
I would bathe in the holy rivers	32	It is the rainy month of Sāvan	182
If bronze or iron or gold breaks	79		
If by going about naked	212	Kabir: a sinner is averse to the love of God	216
If his inner self is full of low cravings	208	Kabir, all men mock at me for my low caste	215
If I keep silent men think me stupid	117	Kabir: I am the worst of men	216
If I remember Him I live	53	Kabir, I cast down mine eyes modestly	217
If I should bring a pitcher	224		
If one smear of blood pollutes a garment	77	Kabir: the cottage of the Saint is comfortable	216
If the mind is unclean, all else is unclean	133	Kabir: there are very few men indeed	216
Ignorance pervadeth all creatures	89	Kabir: what good does it do you to have given up	217
In a dream, I was lifted high towards Him	204	Kabir, where there is divine knowledge there is righteousness	217
In Asāḍ the sun scorches	109		
In error and illusion I have passed many lives	244	Kabir, why, O Mullah, climbest thou up to thy minaret	217
In search of a true saint	256	Know this the way of the Yoga	100
In the body, God is present	237	Knowledge of the Transcendent is not to be obtained	129
In the company of the Saints	161		
In the forge of continence	51		
In the house in which men sing the Lord's praises	60	Let compassion be thy mosque	77
		Let knowledge of God be thy food	46
In the realm of Grace, spiritual power is supreme	50	Let my tongue become a hundred thousand tongues	47
In the vat of the body	249		

		PAGE
Let no man be proud because of his caste		136
Let the rains come down in torrents, Lord		222
Like the holy, the ever-flowing waters of the sacred Ganges		264
Listen My heart		71
Listen, my sisters, to the sound of the rain		93
Listen, O fortunate ones, to my joyful Song		131
Lord, Creator and Truth		57
Lord, I am Thy Child		148
Lord, Thou lettest not Thy servants		188
Lord, Thou mighty River, all-knowing, all seeing		69
Lost in the maze of falsehood		110
Lust and wrath waste the body		98
Lust thou native of hell		202
Man flingeth away a ruby		159
Man, thou art a herdsman, pausing at a pastureland		176
Man, thou dwellest in the world that is as a pool		58
Manifest in all things He is also Unmanifest Ground		172
Many Shastras, many Simrities have I seen		158
Maya, the mythical goddess		46
Mind, thou art a spark of Divine Light		131
Mortal man, what has been Thy profit		234
My eyes are wet with the Lord's nectar		146
My friends, discard the devices of worldly wisdom		169
My mind is pierced with the Name of God		74
My own system is constant		101
Nānak, among millions of men		166
Nānak, burn in the fire		124
Nānak; such are the blasphemers		76

		PAGE
Nānak, the man of divine knowledge		132
Neither gods nor demigods nor men endure		80
Neither the lunar nor the solar spheres		81
No mortal man lives long enough to exhaust his desires		119
Noble birth and great fame		75
Not cast down by sorrow		209
Not to be grasped or sounded is the living God		161
Nothing can bar or mar the paths		36
Now, the Lord is my last refuge		147
O babīhā, wail not and cry not for water		137
O black buck, listen to me		89
O Covetousness, misled by thee		203
O Lord, in Thee I have taken refuge		201
O Lord, Nānak hath taken refuge in Thee		160
O Lord of men and of creatures		173
O lotus flower green was thy stalk		118
O man, nothing shall go with thee		171
O man, practise asceticism after the following manner		271
O Master come to me		111
O mine eyes it was the Lord who gave ye Light		130
O my Beloved, sleep hath fled from me		193
O my body, what hast thou brought to pass		130
O my foolish friend		68
O my mind, abide thou ever with God		126
O my soul, why art thou busy and troubled		55
O my True Lord, what is there		126
O peace-giving night, prolong thyself		185
O people of the city everyone knows		232

285

	PAGE		PAGE
O Self-love, Self-will, thou root of births and deaths	203	Six the systems, six their teachers	61
O Servant of God, True Guru	54	Soiled by its former births the soul is black as jet	134
O Soul thou dost not abide by the Guru's teachings	206	Some call on the Lord 'Ram, Ram!' Some cry 'Khuda!'	193
O Thou who destroyest the pain and grief of the wretched	157	Some make a pact with	145
O worthless and ignorant mortal	159	Some sing hymns without faith and knowledge	116
Of a woman are we conceived	93	Sword, that smiteth in a flash	270
Of all Religions this is the best Religion	158	Tears trickle down from my eyes	239
Of all the lights in the courtyard	195	Tell me in what street I shall find my Beauteous Lord	147
Of him who truely believes in the Name	35	That Being is Pure; He is without stain	56
Of His bounty one cannot write enough	42	That man in whom there never kindles	210
On hearing of the Lord (Evening Prayer)	52	That man is blind within and blind without	194
One man by shaving his head	268	That man who in the midst of grief is free from grieving	207
One may read cartloads of books	91	The body thou smearest with sandal paste	242
Only a fool listens to an ignorant fool	136	The disciple who serves at the Guru's feet	170
Our Saviour saveth	185	The drop of water is in the sea	97
Our transgressions are past counting	138	The fact that the skies are without limit	79
Out of the cotton of compassion	92	The final vision of justice is not with Man	81
Perversity of the soul is like a woman of low caste	76	The firmament is Thy salver	61
Pilgrimages, penances, compassion and almsgiving	40	The flesh hath five weaknesses	84
Pleasant is the month of Jeth	108	The grave lies at the end of the road	80
Priceless are His attributes	43	The hard of heart	144
Primal Being, sublimely beautiful	240	The Lord first created Light	215
		The Lord God is King	89
Rejoice with me, O mother	126	The Lord hath entered my being	113
Repose, peace, wealth, the nine treasures	174	The Lord is the Truth Absolute	30
		The Maker and Ground of all things is the one Lord	167
Save this world consumed in fire	135	The man who knoweth God cannot have a price set on him	165
Self-will is opposed to the Holy Name	133		
She whose heart is full of love	114	The man who knoweth God clingeth to God	163
Sins abound in me	263		

286

	PAGE		PAGE
The man who knoweth God is called Brahm-gyanī	164	They who abandon God, the Giver of all things	160
The man who knoweth God is the Creator of the universe	165	This age is like a drawn Sword	82
The month of Maghar is bliss	112	This in my heart have I realised	260
The nectar laved glance of Guru Angad	254	This is the greatest sickness of the soul	67
The nose-string of life is in the master's hands	121	Those who appear great men in the world's eyes	182
The One God is the Father of all	187	Those who believe in power	30
The path of the Saint is the strange path	128	Those who have destroyed self-will and live in humility	168
The Saint seeth the Light of the Lord in all things	173	Those who have inner belief in the Name	36
The sea of life is hard to cross	99	Those who, impure within, seem pure outwardly	129
The season of rain has come	109	Those who, pure within, are also pure without	129
The self-centred man from the start took the wrong path	144	Those whom God has chosen	253
The shell of the egg of delusion has burst	195	Thou art my Father	180
The snake sloughs its old skin	225	Thou art the Lord; to Thee we pray	159
The souls whom the Guru has enlightened	140	Thou art the only one within us and without us	142
The tresses that adorned these lovely heads	87	Thou hast acquired this human frame	58
The True Guru, the divine One, is without enmity	137	Thou hast cleansed the dirt from thy heart	246
The Vedic scholars have handed down to us	122	Thou hast stated the problem correctly	99
The Word of God shall be everlasting	210	Though a man on earth do evil deeds	183
There are hundreds of thousands of worlds	41	Though Khurāsān has been shielded by Thee	86
There are those who profess one thing and practise another	160	Though my body be crippled with disease	78
There can be no peace for man	168	Though the outer walls of the palace be made of pearls	65
There is a place called City-of-no-Sorrows	230	Through belief in the Name	35
There is no counting fools, the morally blind	38	Through His Will He creates all the forms of things	29
There is no counting of men's prayers	37	Through uncountable ages	103
There is one God (Japji: Morning Prayer)	28	Thus spake God unto me	270
These are the secrets of True husbandry	95	Thy Name, O Lord, is my sustenance	127
They are not truly husband and wife	135	Thy praisers praise Thee	41
		Thy riches will not go with thee	171
		To me who am like a blind man	227

	PAGE		PAGE
To remember the Lord is the highest religious duty	157	When the Guru is on one's side	259
Trust not the avaricious man	139	When under a sullen sky	117
		Where is the gate, where the mansion	44, 52
Vast and without bounds are the waters of the Ocean	70	Where Self exists	106
		Where thou couldst not be saved	157
We are set apart from Thee	181	Whither need I go to seek holiness	233
Wearing the armour of concentration	257	Who frighteneth none	209
Were a man to live through the four ages	32	Who knoweth God dwelleth undisturbed in the love of God	164
Were a thousand moons to arise	121	Who knoweth God is, of the pure, the purest	163
Were my span of life to extend to a million years	66	Who knoweth God liveth ever unattached	162
What does it profit you	268	Who knoweth God maketh himself the dust	163
What is the source of thy knowledge	102	Why call them blind	122
What is the use of rich food and fine clothes	78	Why forget Him	172
		Why hast thou left thy home	101
What pleases the Lord	111	With lust and with anger	62
What would it matter that they rent my body	231	With the beginning of the breath of life	102
When a man's mind entertains vanity	183	With the coming of spring	137
		Without true love there is no honour	127
When a man is in dire straits	176	Wrath, pitiless and seed of strife	202
When God made this illusion, the world	172		
When I see my Beloved Guru I live	190	Ye have no power to speak or in silence listen	48
When I think of myself	231	Ye, who seek after Truth, caste down your vanity	206
When the hands, feet and other parts	39		